Teachers College Studies in Education

THE NATURE OF
Nondirective Group Psychotherapy

An Experimental Investigation

LEON GORLOW, Ph.D.
ASSISTANT PROFESSOR OF PSYCHOLOGY
SYRACUSE UNIVERSITY

ERASMUS L. HOCH, Ph.D.
CLINICAL PSYCHOLOGIST
LYONS V. A. HOSPITAL

EARL F. TELSCHOW, Ed.D.
ASSISTANT PROFESSOR OF PSYCHOLOGY
UNIVERSITY OF ROCHESTER

BUREAU OF PUBLICATIONS
TEACHERS COLLEGE · COLUMBIA UNIVERSITY
NEW YORK · 1952

FOREWORD

Group methods of psychotherapy have gained widespread acceptance during the past decade. Clinical experience has verified what
personality theory would lead us to expect—that the group is a
psychologically potent setting for the working out of personal problems. The effectiveness of group therapy challenges inquiry. What
is it about the group situation that is at once reassuring, stimulat-
ing, healing? What must a group leader do to make this coming
together of people a therapeutic experience rather than a forum?
What benison is there in the discovery of shared hurts and fears?
How many therapists are there in a group, really—one who is so
designated, or are there as many givers of help as there are re-
ceivers? What is the nature of the process, the role of the leader,
the relationship of members? Such questions as these are examined
in this book. Gorlow, Hoch, and Telschow here report the results
of the first major research investigation of this new approach to
working with troubled people.

The authors of this book bring to their task considerable clinical
acumen. They also bring to bear in their analysis of group therapy
the techniques of controlled inquiry. One of the criteria of the
maturity of a field of investigation is the extent to which the data
of the field can be given significant quantitative expression.
Earlier clinical studies of group therapy, valuable as they have been
in revealing the promise of the method and in identifying hypotheses, leave the problem without precise statement and the hypotheses without objective check. Our understanding of group psychotherapy, broadened by the research reported in this volume, should
grow apace as other investigators subject their clinical work to
rigorous quantitative treatment.

There is, of course, no virtue in correlations, chi-squares, and
t-tests apart from the purposes for which they are used. Statistical
methods have most meaning when they are used to check on hy-

potheses drawn from a consistent theory. The investigation reported in these pages is cast within the framework of nondirective or client-centered therapy, testing a number of hypotheses that arise when the theory is applied to the workings of groups. The theory provides coherence to the study, and the results have significance not alone for group work but for the theory in general. Although the authors are aware of the limitations of their data and are modest in their conclusions, an observer can point out their impressive achievement in moving group therapy from the realm of clinical impressions to the realm of testable, theory-related hypotheses, while making the theory itself come to life in their application of it.

It is fitting that a study of group therapy should itself be a group enterprise. There is growing recognition in our time that research is among the things that people can often do better in groups than alone. It is likely that the close association of these three men in their research resulted in a level of achievement, a kind of creativity, exceeding that which they could have achieved working alone. Certainly they helped each other to be better therapists, and they sustained each other through hundreds of hours of arduous tabulating and analyzing of data. Possibly a major contribution of their work is the demonstration of how rewarding such a group undertaking can be.

NICHOLAS HOBBS

ACKNOWLEDGMENT

The authors wish to express their sincere appreciation to Dr. Laurance F. Shaffer, Dr. Helen M. Walker, and Dr. Gertrude P. Driscoll who gave valuable assistance in the development of this study. They are particularly indebted to Dr. Nicholas Hobbs, who guided the thinking of the authors throughout the entire research. Sincere gratitude is likewise due the group members who permitted a study of their personal problems in the cause of advancing the state of knowledge of the group psychotherapy process.

For any errors of omission or commission in the execution of the study itself the authors assume responsibility.

L. G.
E. L. H.
E. F. T.

CONTENTS

THE NATURE OF
NONDIRECTIVE GROUP PSYCHOTHERAPY

CHAPTER I

INTRODUCTION

A source of challenging interest to many clinical psychologists, psychiatrists, and social workers is the problem of group psychotherapy. Practically, group psychotherapy is a process whereby people can resolve their personal difficulties to find more satisfactory modes of adjustment to others as well as to themselves. As differentiated from individual psychotherapy, the process enables individuals to work out their relationships and problems in the realistic atmosphere of social interaction, and thus supplies a context wherein people can relate to each other. Although the method was adopted primarily as a matter of expedience during the last war, the feeling now is that group therapy has values quite beyond that of mere convenience. Group belonging, group reassurance, and the knowledge that others are struggling with problems may have therapeutic value. Although the broad canvas of group therapy can be sketched in such terms, there is little available evidence to suggest a deeper understanding of its issues based upon quantitative study proceeding from theoretical considerations.

The success of recent investigations into the nature of the individual psychotherapy process has affirmed the feasibility as well as the fruitfulness of research in this area. In consequence of the earlier efforts various methods for analyzing protocol data have been shown to be practicable. Categories for classifying verbal behavior have been devised; judges, using such categories, have been able to analyze therapy protocols with a high degree of agreement; statistical treatment of therapy sessions thus quantified has been adjudged appropriate.

As a result of the prior work two courses seem indicated for further research. The investigative techniques which have been found applicable would appear to merit elaboration, and their

1

extension to wider areas seems in order. The present study attempts to realize both these aims. Employing as a point of departure the techniques of analysis already available, it endeavors with appropriate modifications to extend this type of investigation into the area of group psychotherapy, where there is little controlled research.

More particularly, the present study attempts to verify or refute hypotheses deduced from the personality theory associated with nondirective psychotherapy. This theoretical position has most recently been stated by Snygg and Combs [90],* although its source is a large body of research literature [61, 70, 72]. Essentially, the theory professes the basic human need to be the preservation and enhancement of the self. A central concept is the perceiving organism whose behavior follows upon its private conceptions. Perception is need-influenced in the sense that it serves the end of preservation (defense) and self-enhancement, and behavior change is to be understood as deriving from changes in perception. When the theory is translated into the therapeutic hour, the aim of the therapist becomes one of enabling the client to surrender his need to defend himself. As a consequence of reduced threat, the client achieves a different perception of himself and his world. It is in such an unique situation that client perception changes.

The situation which obtains in nondirective group psychotherapy may be described more concretely as follows. According to the therapeutic philosophy of Rogers [67], an individual, given a suitable opportunity in the form of a completely permissive situation, has within himself the potentialities for alleviating his difficulties. Nondirective group psychotherapy is the application, on a group rather than an individual basis, of this system of therapy. In a group of several people discussing their personal difficulties, the therapist attempts to further this common aim with a minimum of direction. He endeavors to convey his sympathetic understanding and genuine acceptance of the members' emotionalized attitudes. The members meanwhile respond to each other and the therapist in whatever fashion their needs dictate. Whatever gain accrues is presumed to stem from two sources: (*a*) the free interchange of feelings and attitudes in a thoroughly permissive atmos-

---

* Numerals in brackets refer to numbered items in the Bibliography, pp. 114–19.

phere; (*b*) the constant opportunity of the group members to measure themselves against a stable reference point, the consistence of the therapist's behavior.

Generally, group psychotherapy has hardly been studied systematically. Relevant testable hypotheses need to be subjected to controlled analysis with a view toward reaching conclusions which may be stated at more acceptable levels of confidence than those which arise from clinical observation. Shaffer's [79] statement that "The need to improve our psychotherapy is so great that ultimate gain would probably accrue if all psychologists stopped the practice of therapeutic counseling for the next few years and devoted their entire energies to research designed to increase the value of the process" is not to be dismissed lightly when one considers that the rich speculation in the literature of group therapy has not yet been appreciably tested by controlled methods. Theoretical formulation and speculation are necessarily antecedent to research study. Lately, however, the derivation of techniques for the quantification of therapy protocols has opened new vistas for the research worker and controlled study is now possible.

The scope of many problems in psychology has suggested a need to psychologists which has been expressed recently by Marquis [50] and Rogers [66]. Both have recognized the appropriateness of, and perhaps urgency for, cooperative research. The present study represents such research in nondirective group psychotherapy. The entire problem was considered of such broad scope as to be susceptible of investigation in three areas: the dynamics of the process, the therapeutic role-playing of the participant members, and the activity of the group leader. A research team of three investigators was organized.

It is apparent that an investigation organized along the lines of the present study must have definite limitations. The selectivity of the population, the few groups, the limited number of sessions, the many uncontrollable variables all serve to limit sharply the deductions which can justifiably be made. Even more severe are the statistical limitations. It will be noted, for example, that the number of hypotheses examined is disproportionately large in relation to the relatively small number of subjects. Further, as the study was designed, these subjects were admittedly not drawn at random from a predefined universe. Such elements as willingness to cooperate, for example, imply that generalizations can be made only for a rather restricted, hypothetical universe and that one may only speculate as to how well the findings will apply to a more general universe.

In defense of the project, however, it will be noted that the conclusions which emerge are rather carefully circumscribed. The writers have sought to confine generalizations within proper limits and to draw inferences with suitable reservations. Above all, it must be stressed that it is the intent of the investigators to furnish clues about group therapy which may merit further intensive research rather than to present definitive findings.

CHAPTER II

REVIEW OF THE LITERATURE

A research investigation usually proceeds from those events which have preceded it, and the hypotheses which are developed can be ordered logically in a body of knowledge. It is this historical, cumulative effort that may distinguish science from art. In the past few decades an impressive amount of literature has accumulated pertaining to group psychotherapy. Only recently, however, have techniques been developed which provide quantitative methods for controlled approaches to the complex problem of group psychotherapy. The considerable literature is not organized into an area for research study, and the bulk of the reporting represents, in the main, a large body of unsystemized opinion, suggestion, and conflicting views. The writings, however, are rewarding to the research investigator, for they provide a rich source of hypotheses about the phenomena of therapy based upon the intensive clinical observations of many psychiatrists, psychologists, and case workers.

On the other hand, for a study to be characterized as a research paper, one would prefer that there be stated an *a priori* hypothesis derived from some theoretical view and that this hypothesis be then tested and held to be tenable or untenable within the limits of the experimental design. The relatively late development of quantitative methods for approaching the problems of group psychotherapy has delayed such research.

Although it would have been more appropriate to view the present study in the context of a larger and more clearly defined research area, the character of the literature in group psychotherapy defeats the goal. Instead, this investigation can be viewed as an extension of the limited beginnings of an area for research in non-directive group psychotherapy. The present review of the literature, then, is provided rather as perspective for viewing the present

5

study than as ordering of crucial issues. The aim is to present a general overview of reports in group psychotherapy, followed by a review of studies which tend to the utilization of controlled and quantitative methods.

An overview of the literature discloses the fact that the available articles fall conveniently into three rather natural groupings. People have made contributions of an essentially speculative nature; projects have been carried out and conclusions drawn empirically; finally, attempts have been made recently to subject the group psychotherapy process to more rigorous types of scientific analysis. Thus, it might be said that some people have thought about group therapy, others have tried it out, still others have studied it. That each of these orientations serves a function, although certain shortcomings are apparent, will be shown in the following sections.

SPECULATION ABOUT GROUP PSYCHOTHERAPY

In order that the diversity of views in the literature may be represented, it has been necessary to adopt a somewhat arbitrary organization. The classification which seemed most fitting was a threefold one, dividing the thinking about the group therapy process into (a) structure; (b) function; (c) phenomena.

Structure

Meiers' [52] statement that group therapy "has a long Past but a short History" aptly characterizes the distinction between its unwitting utilization through the ages and the more recent conscious application of standardized group techniques. While the historical origins of a therapeutic kind of group interaction reside in rite, drama, folklore, and the like, the term "group psychotherapy" has been coined as recently as 1931 to designate the current practice of group treatment.

Transitional between the two eras is the period ushered in by Pratt's [60] attempt in 1906 to employ mass instruction for the treatment of tubercular patients. From these modern roots grew a series of similar efforts to use the force of group interaction in achieving therapeutic ends [13, 15, 87]. These early attempts at practicing group therapy, concerned mainly with the treatment of psychosomatic difficulties, soon gave way to efforts to treat the more directly emotional difficulties. Thus, Hadden [31] employed the class technique in the treatment of neuroses, and Lazell [46] attempted group treatment of dementia praecox.

A natural consequence of this historical development has been the recent attempt on the part of several schools of psychological thought to adapt group psychotherapy to their respective doctrines and philosophies. Consequently, as now practiced, group treatment ranges all the way from a highly structured didactic situation, through a classical analytic technique, to Slavson's [82] "permissive" groups, and finally to a nondirective approach, with which this study concerns itself.

Several writers have devised systems of classifying group treatment techniques. Thomas [94], for example, sees group psychotherapy as falling into two broad types—the analytic and the repressive-inspirational—constituting the two ends of a continuum along which the various group psychotherapies can be arranged. Sarlin and Berezin [71] conceive the problem in somewhat similar fashion. From his own frame of reference, Moreno [55] sees the alternatives of a confessional approach and a nonconfessional approach. Finally, Meiers [52] orders all group therapies under two headings—the leader-centered didactic approach and the member-centered dramic approach.

A conscious concern with the more practical aspects of group therapeutic systems is currently noticeable. To cite one such factor —that of group composition—one may note the following divergent views. Wender [98] holds that "Insofar as possible, groups should be planned so that they are fairly homogeneous in intellectual and social backgrounds." Cohen [16], on the other hand, feels that a calculated attempt should be made to include varied personality types in the composition of each group, namely, one or two outspoken or aggressive individuals, several mature and stable personalities, and several depressed, anxious members.

One may note two further moot questions. Should the group be "closed" or "open," that is, is its composition to remain unchanged, or are new members to be admitted as others drop out during the therapy cycle? Should the procedure be fixed or should it be flexible? With respect to both of these questions conjecture abounds [51, 93, 97].

Function

Until recently, group psychotherapy has been regarded as serving the function of expedience, finding justification in such terms as economy of time and conservation of personnel. Only gradually has this attitude yielded to the notion that group therapy has advantages inherent in it and can be regarded as a therapeutic technique in its own right. The latter recognition appears in such statements as that of Blackman [11] that "A setting is provided where the patient finds it possible to re-evaluate his concepts" and that of Schilder [74] that "In a group the patients realize with astonishment that the thoughts which have seemed to isolate them are common to all of them."

The changing functions assigned group therapy over the years are succinctly summarized by Foulkes [24], who sees the successive views of group treatment as follows: (a) the narrowest view—group therapy as a timesaver; (b) a less narrow view—group therapy as a substitute for individual therapy; (c) a broader view —group therapy as "a new method of therapy, investigation, information, and education"; (d) the broadest view—group therapy as "an expression of a new attitude toward study and improvement of human interrelations in our time."

It seems only natural that this concern with establishing the real function of group psychotherapy should have pointed up the further issue designated by Shaskan [80] in the title of his article, "Must Individual and Group Psychotherapy Be Opposed?" The consensus of current thinking is best represented by a quotation from Klapman [40]: ". . . group psychotherapy, since it employs a different principle in treatment, may not be an exactly collateral substitute for individual therapy and a secondary choice, but rather . . . may utilize a segment of the psychodynamic and therapeutic spectrum which is not quite so readily engaged by individual therapy."

Phenomena

Relevant to the hypotheses tested in this study are the speculations concerning the "dynamics" of the group therapy process. The efforts to account for phenomena involve more often than not a recourse to psychoanalytic theory. What the present study attempts to demonstrate, among other things, is that several of the more significant process dynamics can be adequately understood in terms of specified, measurable variables without the necessity of invoking debatable symbolic concepts.

While some writers, such as Pederson-Krag [57], for example, hint that the phenomena which occur are in large measure dependent upon the type of group set up, others, among them Braceland [12], feel that ". . . the laws which govern group action, cohesion, and stratification are applicable to all groups." Without attempting at the moment to assess the correctness of either of these positions, the following paragraphs present a series of representative speculations concerning the phenomena which allegedly characterize therapeutic group interaction.

Perhaps the most commonly held view of the group therapy process is that which conceives of it in terms of *sibling rivalry behavior.* Typical is the statement of Sarlin and Berezin [71] to the effect that "the therapeutic sessions represented symbolically a family of siblings held together by a common therapeutic need. . . ." A series of similar speculations on the part of other writers in the field indicates a general readiness to postulate such mechanisms as being operative without either feeling an expressed need for the proof of their existence or attempting to account for phenomena in more tangible, observable terms [41].

A similar situation exists with reference to a second phenomenon —*transference*—concerning the role of which there is especially wide agreement among those speculating about what happens in the group therapy process. Klapman [41] offers the hypothesis that "One of its [group therapy's] principal effects is to quicken and expedite the appearance of transference to the therapist and in a commensurate measure also between the various members of the group." Slavson [83], Wender [97], and Redl [65] likewise consider transference an essential feature of group therapy.

However, on a practical level, there is much controversy concerning the quality of transference which should be encouraged. Slavson [85] believes that a negative transference to the leader is desirable. He recognizes, however, that in a group situation the intensity of negative feelings toward the therapist may reach a dangerous peak. Baruch [6], and others employing nondirective therapy, prefer to work with a positive transference to the leader since they feel that members are more likely to feel free to express themselves in such a relationship.

A positive relationship between group members and leader is criticized by Ackerman [2] as fostering dependence and preventing members from expressing aggression. It would seem that Ackerman, like Slavson, believes that release of hostility and aggression is essential for group members to experience gain from therapy. It seems evident that adequate consideration has not been accorded the many variables involved, nor has there been any objective evaluation of what takes place in therapy with a particular type of transference to the leader.

Related to the problem of transference is the phenomenon of *member therapeutic role-playing.* There was early recognition of the member-therapist aspect of the dynamics of group psychotherapy. White [100] in 1932 spoke of "the inter-weaving of emotional streams among people when they are in a group" which bind people who can both modify and be modified by the group. At the 1932 conference on the problem of the "Group Method" of which White was chairman, general agreement prevailed concerning the phenomena of member interaction [10, 32, 54]. More recently, Solby [91], Moreno [53], and Schauer [73] have observed that it is the *group* that is the therapeutic agent as a result of the interactions between individuals who form the group.

In *The Practice of Group Therapy* [85], representing as it does his view of the dynamics of group psychotherapy, Slavson states: "Of no small value is the inter-patient therapy which is fully demonstrated. . . . As a matter of fact much more interpretation, including interpretation of dreams, and insight giving, originates with the patients themselves than with the therapist. Tentative observations seem to point to the conclusion that the more inter-patient therapy occurs, the better. Patients can accept censure, suggestions, interpretation and guidance from each other with less disturbance and hostility than from the therapist." [1]

Beyond theoretical considerations, case reports describe the

_____

[1] S. R. Slavson (Ed.), *The Practice of Group Therapy,* p. 37. New York: International Universities Press, 1947.

behavior of members as therapists more concretely [5, 25]. While some investigators feel strongly that group members provide the participants with effective therapy, other workers are not convinced. Durkin *et al.* [20] have written that "therapeusis comes primarily from each member's relationship with the therapist rather than with the other group members." Lowrey [48] has stated that ". . . the essential point is that the *lines of treatment relationship are from each individual to the therapist.* In other words, this is therapy *in* the group, rather than therapy *by* the group. Group Interaction does occur, and it has a therapeutic effect, but this is definitely a secondary mechanism. . . ." Lowrey says later, however, that "eventually, therefore, it would be group interaction which was the potent therapeutic agent." [2] Wolf [101], on the other hand, has reported himself so thoroughly convinced of the values of member therapeutic behavior as to urge his therapeutic group to meet without him, allowing sub-leader therapists to function freely.

Presently, then, the question of the dynamics of member-therapist behavior remains open and its mechanisms are still to be described with accuracy. A fair generalization, in consideration of the reports in the literature, would be that although the phenomenon of member-therapist behavior has been recognized and stated, there is little precision to the statements and little is known about its actual character.

More knowledge about the events of member-therapist behavior may be useful, for it relates to another problem, viz., the composition of groups. Slavson [85] has declared that "Patients with a common psychological syndrome who have similar personality problems . . . are most helpful to one another, even though their symptoms may differ." And "thus it becomes clear that a therapy group must be specially planned." While he does not present evidence for this form of statement, the present investigators would pose the further question: Should not groups be planned with large consideration to member-therapist behavior, which is in fact a large share of member participation?

A fourth major phenomenon accorded wide attention is that of

[2] L. G. Lowrey, "Group Treatment for Mothers," *American Journal of Orthopsychiatry*, Vol. 14, p. 590.

therapeutic gain. Here, the abundant speculation may be organized under three headings: (*a*) the role of insight in promoting gain; (*b*) the degree of gain on the part of a member who participates only minimally; (*c*) the extent to which personality structure is altered as a function of gain.

With respect to the first of these, the role of insight, there is almost unanimity of opinion as to its importance. Luchins [49], in discussing the purposes of group therapy, lists as primary the imparting of insight into social factors influencing personality development. Schilder [74] and Lazell [45] place similar emphasis on this factor.

Concerning the second consideration, the phenomenon of the passive member, Slavson [83], among others, regards this as an essential feature distinguishing group from individual psychotherapy. Simon *et al.* [81] indeed stress the fact that "there is evidence that passive (non-articulate) participation can be as emotionally intense and as therapeutic as active (articulate) participation."

Finally, concerning the degree of personality alteration involved in therapeutic gain, claims range all the way from a profound reorganization of character structure to a mere scratching of the peripheral layers of personality. Representing the middle ground between these two extremes is the feeling of Glatzer and Durkin [26] that their group relationship therapy ". . . does not attempt to remake individuals according to any set pattern," but endeavors more modestly to help them ". . . to accept themselves and understand their fundamental motivations."

Critique of Speculation Concerning Group Therapy

From even such a necessarily cursory overview it is apparent that there has been no dearth of conjecture relative to the process of group therapy. Indeed, from this mass of speculation has emerged an abundance of fruitful hypotheses. At the same time, however, this type of theorizing would seem to have its limitations. For one, it is characterized by the tendency to custom-tailor explanations rather than to explain a process in terms of simple, irreducible elements. Further, simple assertion of an alleged phenomenon is not infrequently regarded as proof *per se* of its existence. Finally, one notes throughout a certain readiness to employ symbolic interpretations before more prosaic explanations have been explored and found wanting. While, then, the tendency to speculate about the group therapy process has been a natural, and in some measure profitable, precursor to actual research, it can hardly be regarded as a suitable substitute for the latter.

GROUP THERAPY PROJECTS

Between the period of speculation and the application of experimental principles to the study of group therapy came the stage during which specific projects were undertaken and conclusions drawn empirically. The fact that these projects were carried out under at best semi-controlled conditions resulted in deductions of an essentially clinical rather than scientific nature. Since this type of tentative experimentation did, however, set the stage for more rigorously controlled investigation, its consideration is appropriate.

In the interest of presenting a somewhat systematic overview of the group therapy projects reported in the literature, it is necessary to arrange their number under appropriate headings. The following sections, therefore, treat group therapy as having been attempted: (*a*) with various populations; (*b*) with various media; (*c*) with various techniques; (*d*) for various purposes.

Populations

Group therapy projects range from Alpert's [4] application of group psychotherapy principles in the treatment of a class of kindergarten children to Kolodney's [43] attempt to resolve the personality difficulties of mothers on a group basis. Any number of enterprises might be cited to attest the fact that children are as amenable to this type of treatment as are adults. One need but mention as typical examples the activities of Little and Konopka [47], Stewart and Axelrod [93], Solomon and Axelrod [92], and Slavson *et al.* [86].

A second large population found in recent years to be well suited to group psychotherapy is the military. Among others, Hobbs and Pascal [36] employed group therapy at an Army Air Force convalescent hospital, while Abrahams and McCorkle [1] carried out a group psychotherapy program at an Army rehabilitation center. Grotjahn [28] and Hadden [29] conducted similar projects.

The projects of Lawlor [44], Baruch [6], and Kadis and Lazarsfeld [38] offer some idea of the additional diverse populations amenable to group psychotherapeutic treatment.

Media

Although direct verbal communication is the principal medium in interview group therapy, it is interesting to note the variety of devices employed in facilitating and promoting such verbal interaction. Schwartz [77] found, for example, that a group showing of combat films was instrumental in promoting a release of feeling in therapy subsequent to such an experience. In a related experiment Rubin and Katz [69] found a group of psychotic depressives much more amenable to therapy after a showing of auroratone films to groups of five to ten, two or three times a week. Similarly intent upon employing a "loosening-up" technique, Horwitz [37] used the "spontaneous drama" as a medium for promoting free release of feeling preparatory to group discussion. Finally, Curran and Schilder [18] and Bender [9] discovered the value of puppetry in making subsequent group discussion periods more fruitful.

Techniques

An important group leader technique is that of setting the therapeutic atmosphere and giving definition to the working relationships within the group. It is unfortunately true that this so-called structuring technique is seldom mentioned in the literature. Foulkes [23], an exponent of psychoanalytic group therapy, advocates a minimum of instructions or rules during the first session. He believes that minimal structuring results in a maximum of freedom in self-expression. Baruch [6], employing nondirective techniques, tends to agree with the analytic position but advocates introducing a few essential mechanics in the initial session defining the discussion method. Most writers agree that freedom of expression should be encouraged during the first session and some attempt made to explain the nature of the experience. However, it is seldom that the literature contains explicit details concerning structuring techniques in group therapy with adequate criteria for their use.

How much should a group leader participate? This is perhaps the greatest single problem in group psychotherapy. If he participates extensively, social interaction among the members is limited and the experience is apt to become similar to individual therapy. On the other hand, if he participates minimally, the meetings may take on the character of a "bull session" with consequent argumentativeness rather than an atmosphere of sympathetic understanding.

Baruch [6] found it profitable to turn leadership over gradually to the members as the sessions progressed. This would seem to indicate a conviction that the interaction of the members is at least as important as the activity of the therapist.

Klapman [41] feels that group therapy calls for more active participation on the part of the therapist to prevent undesirable transferences from developing between members. However, the reader is at a loss to discover what is explicitly meant by "more active participation." This lack of definition seems to indicate that the extent and timing of leader participation rest solely upon clinical experience and intuitive leader feelings.

The extent and quality of therapist participation in group therapy changes, according to Slavson [82], as the sessions progress. He advocates, at least with children, a gradual change from the role of complete acceptance and passivity to the more active role of participant who becomes an image of authority and restraint. This change in role, he continues, is determined by the growing maturity of the clients and their increased capacity to cope with reality. These criteria would seem to call for rather shrewd clinical judgment. The lack of more objective definition would seem to leave considerable room for serious error in estimating the psychological readiness of clients to assimilate a changing leader role.

The foregoing theoretical positions concerning the extent of leader participation in group therapy are characterized by: (*a*) conflicting opinions resulting from different frames of reference, and (*b*) lack of careful definition of the criteria advanced. Indeed, it would seem to be an aspect of group psychotherapy worth subjecting to research methods.

Related to the problem of how much a group leader should participate in therapy is the function of pauses and how they should be handled by the therapist. This is another aspect of group therapy which has received remarkably little attention in the literature. Foulkes [23] points out that silences in group therapy have a diversity of meanings. They may indicate expectation, apprehension, resistance, or they may result from a release of tension. His clinical experience has convinced him that a real sex difference exists regarding pauses. It is his feeling that men usually feel more at ease during silences. In the early sessions he attempts to break pauses through the interjection of a comment or interpreting the resistance. Later, however, he allows the members to cope with pauses in their own way. The timing of this change-over is apparently a matter of clinical judgment, since Foulkes does not mention any objective criteria. He concludes by asserting that silences should provoke no apprehension if it is obvious to the group that the leader is not anxious about them. Dewar [19] describes the tension usually inherent in the first group session and states, "It is our practice to break the tension after about five minutes" by throwing in a controversial remark or by querying the silence itself. Apparently the time limit mentioned is arbitrary.

Simply stated, an interpretation is a therapist statement which attempts to explain behavior by pointing out cause and effect relationships in a client's life adjustment of which the client is partially or completely unaware. The desired result, of course, is increased self-understanding and the development of insight.

It is quite apparent that interpretation, if unwisely used, can be a source of considerable threat to a client and may provoke undue anxiety. In view of this, it is surprising to find this important technique rather vaguely defined in the literature and conditions favorable to its use not clearly set forth.

In discussing the appropriate use of interpretation, Ackerman [3] states that it should be employed only when "expressions of specific emotional trends are sufficiently solidified." Schilder [75] asserts that "An interpretation is given to the patient if the situation warrants it." In discussing the role of the leader Glatzer and Durkin [26] point out that the timing of interpretation is of primary importance but finally conclude that it depends on clinical skill.

The effect of the therapist's personality on the total group experience is undoubtedly a tremendously important variable. However, it is one that is exceedingly difficult to control and examine. Slavson [85] believes that a group leader's success largely depends upon "solidity as well as the flexibility of its own personality integration, suitability of temperament, capacity for understanding others, empathic index, knowledge of the complexities of behavior and his training and experience in the specialty."

According to Foulkes [23] the attitude of the group leader is perhaps more important than what he actually says. The therapist should be his natural self, and yet should remain detached so that he does not bring his own problems into the group.

Almost all theories of psychotherapy stress that the therapist should prevent his own value system from being expressed in the course of treatment. An exception to this point of view is that of Schilder [76], who maintains that this is impossible inasmuch as a body of knowledge (psychoanalysis) has in itself a moral point of view and practically forces definite action by the therapist.

It is apparent that the above writers recognize the importance of the leader's personality as it affects group psychotherapy. However, the lack of consistency in their views, and the apparent need for precise measurement of the factors involved, point up the necessity for research studies oriented around this important variable.

Although the literature contains a variety of assumptions and speculations concerning the leader's role in different types of interview group therapy, there seems to be an awareness that verification through empirical investigation or research studies is essential.

Purposes

Only four articles have been selected in this connection, but the diversity of their nature gives some indication of the varied purposes to which the method has been adapted.

Klapman [40] employs group psychotherapy as a convenient entering wedge for establishing transference with psychotics which can be utilized in the individual therapy session. By allowing each client in the group session to act in a sense as a therapist for other members, he succeeds in getting the client "on his side" in that the client conceives of himself as a co-worker of the therapist.

Somewhat akin to training analysis is the purpose to which Hadden [30] put group therapy in teaching its principles to a group of physicians. Serving as members of groups, observing other groups in progress, and later conducting groups themselves, the physicians obtained a more intimate knowledge of the principles of group psychotherapy than would otherwise have been possible.

Baruch and Miller [7] demonstrated that group psychotherapy as an adjunct in treating allergy cases could be instrumental not only in resolving the personality difficulties of the group members but in actually decreasing the incidence of allergic symptoms.

Using a kind of educational group therapy with kindergarten children of a progressive school, Alpert [4] succeeded by this device in combating an excessive use of scatological language by the children, finding in the process not only a disappearance of symptoms but a definite improvement in social relationships as well.

Critique of Empirical Deductions from Group Therapy Projects

The basing of conclusions on projects rather than on pure speculation was admittedly a step forward. It introduced an element of objectivity that had previously been lacking. By the same token, however, the new tendency carried with it certain risks. For one thing, this type of experimentation minimized its methodological limitations to a degree which lent it an almost spurious kind of scientific respectability. Moreover, many of the projects give the impression of having served more the purpose of confirming preconceived notions than of testing impartially *a priori* hypotheses. It remained for the stage next to be described to remedy these defects.

CONTROLLED RESEARCH

Only recently has it been demonstrated—largely as a result of the efforts of the nondirective school—that the therapeutic process yields to scientific analysis. Although the results of such investigation are still regarded in many quarters with a certain skepticism, the fact remains that its feasibility has been established.

Studies such as the present, then, owe their existence in large measure to the prior work in individual nondirective psychotherapy which has served both to demonstrate the fruitfulness of this type of research and to furnish a methodology upon which to build. Thus, for example, the categories of protocol analysis employed by Porter [59], Royer [68], Snyder [88], and Curran [17] have constituted convenient points of departure. Similarly, Raimy's [62] successful investigation of the self-concept has offered the additional assurance that such protocol analysis preserves with sufficient fidelity the essence of the therapeutic process to make its investigation on more abstract levels defensible. Finally, the recently published "parallel studies" project under the coordination of Raskin [63], by emphasizing the utility of and need for cooperative investigation in this area, has lent the present study additional reason for being.

When the literature is reviewed for instances of this type of controlled research, one is struck by its absence. A survey of the published material yields only three papers which tend in the direction of scientific analysis as against empirical study.

In the earliest of these Hobbs and Pascal [36] attempted to contrast the respective effectiveness of three group approaches—authoritarian, eclectic, and nondirective. Using verbatim typescripts of group sessions, they assigned client and counselor responses appropriate categories of analysis, dividing the latter into therapeutically positive and negative forms of verbal behavior. On this basis the eclectic and nondirective approaches were judged therapeutically more fruitful than the authoritarian.

Proceeding with a somewhat different aim, Fleming and Snyder [22] undertook the task of ascertaining whether measurable changes in personal and social adjustment occurred as a consequence of group play therapy. Choosing two groups of children from the same population—an experimental and a control group —the investigators administered pre- and post-therapy tests with a view to determining whether the group who had received therapy exhibited appreciable changes as a consequence of this experience which the control group had missed. The conclusion was drawn that measurable personality changes did occur.

More closely allied to the present investigation is the recent study of nondirective group psychotherapy by Peres [58]. Using as data six recorded sessions of a therapy group consisting of seven graduate students with a major interest in counseling and psychotherapy, Peres analyzed the protocols with two major aims: (a) establishing the relationship between verbal expression and gain; (b) ascertaining the degree of similarity between the group and individual psychotherapy processes. With the aid of categories of protocol analysis taken largely from those used in prior individual nondirective therapy research, the author found "decided differences" between benefited and nonbenefited members.

While Peres' study represents a thoroughgoing attempt to achieve objectivity, attention must be directed to several shortcomings which the present study has sought to remedy. In the first place, the factor of gain with which Peres' study is primarily concerned rests solely upon the subjective opinion of the members —neither the experimenter's clinical estimate of gain nor objective measures thereof enter the picture. That the latter is possible has already been demonstrated by Klopfer [42] and especially by Muench [56], even though the more recent findings of Carr [14] suggest that such measures must be evaluated with proper precautions. Secondly, the use of psychologically sophisticated members whose participation hinges partly on curiosity concerning the experience introduces an element of artificiality. Thirdly, six sessions constitute a rather limited sample of group therapy behavior, all the more so when analysis proceeds largely by means of averages, percentages, and graphs, conclusions being unhindered by tests of significance. Finally, perhaps the most serious limitation of Peres' and prior investigations is the adoption, almost in their entirety, of protocol analysis methods quite adequate for the study of individual therapy but by the same token somewhat ill-suited for the full investigation of the unique group therapy process.

Without attempting to disclaim indebtedness to the previous research, the present investigators have set forth these alleged shortcomings simply by way of indicating the limitations which this study has been designed to circumvent in some degree. Perceiving these latter controlled researches essentially as the culmination of earlier speculative and investigative efforts, the present study attempts to carry the process one step further.

CHAPTER III

THE PROCEDURE

In view of the small number of subjects and the large number of hypotheses, the aim of the joint investigation was to provide tentative answers rather than definitive findings with respect to three comprehensive questions. How are the characteristic aspects of the therapist's behavior conditioned by and influential upon the members' behavior? What are the features which characterize the therapeutic interrelationship of the members among themselves? What are the characteristic attributes of the process as a function of specifiable variables? A prerequisite of the procedure to be adopted, therefore, was that it lend itself to the kind of analysis upon which the answers to these broad questions was dependent.

This chapter sketches the general method and preliminary treatment of the data. The first section describes the plan of the research, while the second sets forth the analysis of data which had to be accomplished before *a priori* hypotheses could be tested.

THE GENERAL METHOD

In skeleton form, the general procedure involved selecting the subjects, providing them with a nondirective group psychotherapy experience, and examining them before and after the experience with certain psychological tests.

The Subjects

Subjects were drawn from the graduate student body of Teachers College, Columbia University. The first step in selection involved announcements in several large classes (several hundred individuals enrolled in each) that group psychotherapy would be available to those who felt the need and desire to use a group experience in an attempt to resolve their personal difficulties.

Those students were urged to respond who felt a genuine need for psychotherapy as distinct from those who might understandably have only intellectual curiosity about the process. Classes were chosen which contained individuals from various areas of specialization, and consequently the groups contained students majoring in science, nursing, elementary education, music, and other fields. Individuals responding to the announcements were given an appointment for an intake interview with one of the three cooperating researchers who were to be the group therapists.

The intake interview served the purpose of determining the motivation of each individual for therapy. The investigators felt that special effort was necessary to insure that candidates for therapy met their criterion for inclusion in the group experience. A candidate for inclusion in a group had to be deeply concerned about some area of personal difficulty. The intake interview was used as a method of testing this concern. Only those were accepted who felt their present life adjustment to be unsatisfactory. Although it had been explicitly stated in the class announcements that the experience was something more than academic activity, as many applicants were rejected for this kind of motivation as were finally selected for the genuineness and disturbing nature of their problems.

Difficulty in concentration, extreme tension when talking before formal groups, doubt about vocational plans, difficulties in parental relationships, and generalized feelings of inadequacy were among the problems of the members. More specifically, one individual reported herself as "neurotic" in the sense that she felt herself "over-reacting to the ordinary stresses and strains" of everyday life. She thought she was anxious too often, perceiving anxiety in a racing heart and profuse perspiration. Her school work suffered, and she could not derive satisfaction from her social relationships. Another person presented himself in an altogether depressed state, characterized by extreme discouragement and resignation. He was deeply concerned over his intense resentment toward his father. Moreover, he perceived himself as completely friendless, and he wondered about his capacity for feeling emotion. A third individual was apparently disoriented and groping. In view of her personality picture, she had been elsewhere informed that her

goal in life was unrealistic. She was struggling against the acceptance of this severely felt limitation. Another individual found
herself obsessed by thoughts of what other people felt toward her;
several others were living in continuous apprehension of the recurrence of "nervous breakdowns." Table 1 provides further identifying data about the group members.

TABLE 1. Identifying Data for the Experimental Population

Age	Sex	Race	Marital Status	Occupation
16–20 (1)	Female (13)	Negro (4)	Divorced (1)	Student (4)
21–25 (8)	Male (4)	White (13)	Widowed (2)	Teacher (3)
26–30 (3)			Married (2)	Nurse (1)
31–35 (2)			Single (12)	Dietitian (1)
36–40 (1)				Housewife (2)
41–45 (2)				Artist (1)
				Musician (1)
				Social worker (2)
				Librarian (1)
				Chemist (1)

Note. Figures in parentheses indicate number of members in each category.

In composing the groups, no consideration was given to various
hypotheses in the literature [39, 85] about proper grouping of
individuals. As many workers in the field deny the importance of
careful grouping as urge its significance. Members were assigned
to groups whose meeting times suited their schedules. Although
the composing of groups is a proper subject for investigation, it is
not within the scope of the present study. Consequently, as Table
1 indicates, the groups were heterogeneous except for the fact that
all the members were pursuing graduate training.

The element of willingness to cooperate, of self-selection by
members for the therapy experience, may mean that generalization
can be made to only a rather restricted, hypothetical universe. On
the other hand, willingness to cooperate and self-selection probably
describe the grand universe of individuals who come to psychotherapy in *any* case. These elements are probably the *sine qua non*
for therapy. Nevertheless, it is important to recognize that the subjects in the present investigation could not possibly be drawn at
random from a predefined universe.

A serious limitation of the study is the number of persons

studied. The investigators are aware of that limitation and of its consequences. Recognition is given to the fact that the study, in a sense, stands midway between clinical observation and a conclusive experiment. In the present investigation, objective clues are derived for further speculation, and it is perhaps well to view the results not as unyielding generalizations but as tentative findings which can lead to hypotheses for future study.

The Experience

Seventeen individuals were finally selected and placed in three groups, each of which was led by one of the cooperating investigators. Group A consisted of three men and three women, Group B of one man and four women, and Group C of six women.

Each group met twice weekly for an hour in nondirective group psychotherapy which, when finally terminated, had afforded twenty sessions to the individuals in Group A, nineteen sessions to those in Group B, and eighteen to Group C.

Nondirective psychotherapy can be characterized by the behavior set for the therapist. The role of the professional therapist in nondirective psychotherapy has been explicitly stated by many workers [34, 67, 89]. Essentially he assumes the position of a non-evaluating, accepting, and permissive individual who does not become a source of threat to generate anxiety and distort perception in the client. His chief aim is to view experience as does his client, who comes to feel that he is understood completely. This is conceived as a unique experience for the individual in personal difficulty and one that is totally different from any he has before encountered. Theoretically, it is within this climate that an individual feels free and safe to explore himself and his world, and reconstitute his perception.

Behavior may be properly classified as nondirective when it does not go beyond the productions of the client at any moment in time. Complete responsibility for the direction of the therapeutic hour remains with the client, and the therapist's role is one of clarifying the content and feeling of his client's immediate remarks. The main specific techniques of nondirective therapy have been named "clarification of feeling," "restatement of content," and "simple acceptance." They correspond to therapist statements of "You're worried this won't turn out" (clarification of feeling), to "You can't find any satisfaction in your work" (restatement of content), to "I see, I understand" (simple acceptance).

Each group leader had received previous supervised training in nondirective therapy with individuals and groups. He was qualified to employ nondirective techniques in accordance with the theoretical constructs of the method.

The Instruments

Since it was necessary to validate certain crucial judgments about the group members in the course of the research and because measurements in some personality variables had to be derived, several instruments were employed. Three psychological tests were selected for use in the investigation and these were administered routinely to each individual both before and after the group experience. After an individually administered Rorschach examination, each group member was required to complete an Incomplete-Sentences Test of fifty items and a Self-Rating Checklist (adapted from Hildreth). Following is a description of each test and its use in the present investigation.

1. *The Rorschach.* The test was administered in the standard fashion. While it had been considered that the Rorschach would be a useful instrument in assessing therapeutic gain, its use for this purpose was abandoned because of conflicting reports from other researches [56, 14, 64]. In a recent investigation, Carr [14] reported that upon quantitative and qualitative study of Rorschachs given before and after therapy, no reliable or consistent changes were apparent. He felt at a loss to explain the discrepancy between his findings and those of Muench [56], and reported on a further study by Reader [64] to further confound the issue. Reader described significant changes in Rorschach protocols, using a new method of Rorschach analysis.

In the present research the Rorschach was employed to validate a ranking of the initial personal adjustment of the group members and to obtain measurements in certain personality variables. In this manner, it was used as an independent criterion for personal adjustment and as a means of deriving *Hostility* and *Anxiety* scores after the method described and validated by Elizur [21].

2. *The Incomplete-Sentences Test.* In this test, the subjects were presented with fifty short phrases to be completed into whole sentences (Appendix B). Bell [8], in reviewing the literature on this form of projective technique, concluded that while the reliability of responses and scoring is not high, they are within the limits of acceptability. He added significantly that the validity of several forms of Incomplete-Sentences is not high enough to suggest their use without other corroborative tests.

Evaluation of the pre-test and post-test was employed as a method of validating judgments of therapeutic gain of each group member. As additional documentation, to heed the counsel of Bell, the Self-Rating Checklist was also evaluated with reference to gain from the therapy experience.

3. *The Self-Rating Checklist.* This test (Appendix C) provided the subjects with an opportunity for self-rating in several areas of feeling and attitude. According to Hildreth [33], these areas provide a yardstick for measuring clinical improvement. In the study, the checklist provided additional evidence for judgment on the members' profit from psychotherapy.

Recently, Thompson [95] found the use of an Incomplete-Sentences Test and a Self-Rating Checklist practicable for yielding significant differences in the extent of attitude change relating to the self-concept. The psychological changes in her subjects followed a six-week experience in the amelioration of their physical appearance. Since these instruments were quite sensitive to relatively small changes in the self-perception of the individual, they were considered useful in estimating the sort of changes that one might expect to emerge from group therapy.

In addition to these instruments a sociometric technique (Appendix D) was devised so that members might evaluate the progress of therapy, their attitudes toward the group leader, and their feelings toward each other. The investigation planned to have these executed by the group members in post-session meetings at regular intervals throughout the course of psychotherapy. However, many of the members reacted negatively to the technique and protested that they were incapable of making the requisite judgments. They were unwilling, for example, to evaluate each other in terms of like, dislike, and degree of upset. The assignment of code numbers to preserve anonymity did not prevent resistance to its use, and it was withdrawn early in the research to preclude the possibility of damaging the therapeutic atmosphere of the groups.

A similar instrument was devised to describe the feelings of the group leader toward the members (Appendix E). The testing of certain hypotheses depended upon a comparison between this group leader blank and the sociometric technique described above. Since the latter had to be withdrawn, the group leader blank could not be used for such a statistical analysis. However, it was decided to utilize it to some extent in a qualitative rather than quantitative manner.

PRELIMINARY TREATMENT OF THE DATA

Before analysis of the data could proceed, three major problems crucial to the research demanded resolution. These were: (*a*) A method for quantifying recorded and transcribed therapy protocols had to be devised. (*b*) The initial personal adjustment of the group members had to be evaluated. (*c*) Members had to be separated into two groups, those who profited most and those who gained little or not at all from psychotherapy. Before *a priori* hypotheses could be tested, it was necessary to have the data yield reliable and valid estimates of these factors.

The Problem of Quantifying Transcribed Therapy Protocols

Although it was thought that a review of other studies in which protocols were quantified would yield a method suitable and immediately applicable to the present data, examination of the investigations of Snyder [88], Curran [17], Porter [59], Peres [58], and others led the present investigators to the conclusion that those methods were inadequate to their purpose. The process of member interaction, the unique phenomenon of group therapy, could not be studied by these methods, and another had to be devised.

This necessity led to the concept of "theme analysis." The concept may be briefly described as follows. In the course of a group therapy session it is customary for one member to assume a more or less central role, the other members focusing upon the expressed problem of this central member and in various ways behaving verbally with relation to it. Verbal activity having this focal point may last for the entire hour, or else, for one reason or another, another member may assume the role of central figure, his expressed problem in turn serving as the focus of interest·for a period of time. Essentially, then, each session consists of one or several such little dramas or subsession wholes, one member assuming a central role and the others behaving in relation to him and his problem. Treating each such unit of verbal activity as a theme to be analyzed, the therapy session becomes a psychologically meaningful configuration.

To define the problem more narrowly, the next step involved an examination of a single theme. It was obvious that there were three broad divisions of communication open to group members. A member could act as "client," as "therapist," or as "participator in general intellectualization." For clarity in exposition, the client categories were designated by the letter C, and the member-therapist and general intellectualization categories by the letters T and G, respectively. Ultimately, twenty-two client categories were identified, while seventeen member-therapist and nine general categories were named (Table 3).

It was apparent that among the categories adopted some could be adjusted superior to others according to certain criteria of verbal behavior. Thus, from the standpoint of good adjustment, such client categories as "Insight and Understanding" and "Positive Attitude Toward Others" could, it seemed, be considered more therapeutic than "Confusion, Asking for Help," or "Negative Attitude Toward Self." By the same token, such general categories as "Comparing Experiences" and "Proposing Course of Group Action" could be deemed more therapeutic than "Asking Group Leader a Question." With reference to the member-therapist categories, it seemed that from the frame of reference of almost every therapeutic system, "Clarification of Feeling" would be judged more therapeutic than "Disapproval, Criticism." These conjectures pointed up the fact that ranking of the categories would furnish a scale of verbal behavior which might greatly facilitate and make more meaningful the subsequent analysis of the data.

By way of establishing such a scale, the three investigators and a fourth person, well versed in the principles of nondirective therapy, ranked the categories from best (most therapeutic) to poorest (least therapeutic) in terms of the adequacy of the verbal behavior represented. Client categories and general categories were ranked from the standpoint of emotional health, while member-therapist categories were ranked in terms of their effectiveness from the frame of reference of nondirective therapy. Table 2 shows the rank order correlation coefficients among the several judges.

TABLE 2. RANK ORDER CORRELATION COEFFICIENTS BETWEEN JUDGES'
RANKING OF 22 CLIENT, 17 MEMBER-THERAPIST,
AND 9 GENERAL CATEGORIES

	Client Categories	Member-Therapist Categories	General Categories
Judges I, II	.95	.83	.85
Judges I, III	.91	.93	.91
Judges I, IV	.74	.74	.79
Judges II, III	.89	.87	.83
Judges II, IV	.72	.73	.75
Judges III, IV	.71	.76	.73

With these coefficients of correlation tending to confirm the appropriateness of this type of verbal behavior scale, the judges arrived, by common agreement, at the ranking of categories to be employed in the analysis of the data. This final ranking is presented in Table 3.

It remained to test the reliability of the coding system. For this purpose, the three cooperating investigators scored two complete group therapy sessions independently and the percentages of agreement between the judges were calculated. Table 4 reports these percentages and the values are sufficiently high to consider the categorization reliable. Since there are several common methods for computing the percentages of agreement between judges, it is important to point out that the procedure followed throughout the study consisted in dividing the number of agreements by the total number of observations. For example, the figure of 75 percent agreement between Judges I and II in Table 4 is derived from their agreement in 339 out of 453 observations.

Finally, it was considered proper that intra-judge reliability over a time interval be calculated. This is given in Table 5, which indicates the percentages of agreement of each judge with himself, after an interval of one month, in coding two complete sessions.

TABLE 3. Final Ranking of Client (C), Member-Therapist (T), and General Intellectualization (G) Categories

[*See Appendix A for definitions*]

C1	Discussion of Plans	T4	Nondirective Lead
C2	Insight and Understanding	T5	Structuring
C3	Positive Attitude Toward Self	T6	Clarifying Question
C4	Positive Attitude Toward Others	T7	Empathy
C5	Ambivalent Acceptance of Self	T8	Approval, Encouragement
C6	Ambivalent Acceptance of Others	T9	Reassurance
C7	Statement of Problem	T10	Opinion
C8	Elaboration of Problem	T10W	Counter-Opinion
C9	Acceptance of Clarification	T11	Requesting Client to Elaborate
C10	Acceptance of Opinion, Advice		(Direct Question, Forcing Client
C11	Acceptance of Interpretation		to Develop)
C12	Ambivalent Acceptance of Clarification	T12	Persuasion, Suggestion, Advice
		T13	Interpretation
C13	Ambivalent Acceptance of Opinion, Advice	T14	Deflection
		T15	Evaluation
C14	Ambivalent Acceptance of Interpretation	T16	Disapproval, Criticism
C15	Rejection of Interpretation	G1	Comparing Experiences
C16	Rejection of Opinion, Advice	G2	Proposing Course of Group Action
C17	Rejection of Clarification		
C18	Confusion, Asking for Help	G3	Posing Question for Group
C19	Defensive Remarks	G4	Giving Information, Answering
C20	Deflection		a Question
C21	Negative Attitude Toward Others	G5	Friendly Discussion
C22	Negative Attitude Toward Self	G6	Intellectual Discussion, Opinion
		G6W	Intellectual Counter-Discussion, Counter-Opinion
T1	Clarification of Feeling		
T2	Restatement of Content	G7	Humor
T3	Simple Acceptance	G8	Asking Group Leader a Question

In essence, a method of protocol classification comprising twenty-two client categories, seventeen member-therapist categories, and nine general intellectualization categories were developed. The method was shown to possess reliability among independent judges and over an interval of time. The fifty-seven recorded and transcribed group therapy sessions comprising approximately twelve hundred pages of single-spaced typescript were then scored into these categories.

The establishment of categories defining group leader behavior involved a similar procedure. Once again the research literature was helpful in selecting certain categories but several more were added to give increased differentiation and definition to leader

TABLE 4. PERCENTAGE OF AGREEMENT BETWEEN JUDGES' CODING OF GROUP
MEMBER CATEGORIES IN TWO GROUP PSYCHOTHERAPY SESSIONS*

	Percent
Judges I, II	75
Judges II, III	85
Judges I, III	70

* 453 responses analyzed.

TABLE 5. PERCENTAGE AGREEMENT OF EACH JUDGE WITH HIMSELF IN ASSIGN-
ING GROUP MEMBER CATEGORIES TO THE SAME TWO SESSIONS
AFTER AN INTERVAL OF ONE MONTH*

	Percent
Judge I, I'	83
Judge II, II'	79
Judge III, III'	81

* 415 responses analyzed.

responses. A rather cursory examination of nondirective group
therapy protocols reveals that practically all group leader responses
may be placed in three main categories: (1) simple acceptance of
client verbalizations, (2) restating of the essential content of the
members' statements, and (3) clarifying of the feelings or attitudes
expressed. In a departure from previous studies, it was decided to
delineate the latter category into still finer descriptions of group
leader clarification of feeling. This will become clear when the
table of group leader categories is discussed.

The final system of group leader categories included twenty-two
different types of responses. To demonstrate that these categories
could be reliably assigned to group therapy protocols, the three researchers independently scored one complete group. The percentages of agreement between the three judges for one complete group
therapy series are given in Table 6.

TABLE 6. PERCENTAGE OF AGREEMENT BETWEEN JUDGES ASSIGNING GROUP
LEADER CATEGORIES IN ONE COMPLETE GROUP THERAPY SERIES

[Figures based on 869 group leader responses]

	Percent
Judges I, II	81
Judges II, III	74
Judges I, III	86

On the basis of the figures in Table 4, it was demonstrated that group leader behavior had been defined adequately enough so that independent judges were able to assign categories to protocol data with considerable reliability. These judges were also asked to determine the direction of leader statements in terms of the member with whom he was apparently interacting; almost perfect agreement resulted.

The final system of group leader categories is presented in Table 7. To the left of each category are the code letters used for scoring and tabulation purposes. Specific examples of leader behavior in each of these categories are given in Appendix A.

TABLE 7. CATEGORIES OF GROUP LEADER BEHAVIOR

SA	Simple Acceptance
RC	Restatement of Content
CF	Clarification of Feeling (General)
CFA	Clarifying a Negative Feeling Expressed Toward Self
CFB	Clarifying a Positive Feeling Expressed Toward Self
CFC	Clarifying an Ambivalent Feeling Expressed Toward Self
CFD	Clarifying a Negative Feeling Expressed Toward Others
CFE	Clarifying a Positive Feeling Expressed Toward Others
CFF	Clarifying Ambivalent Feelings Expressed Toward Others
CFG	Clarifying a Group Feeling
CFH	Clarifying Divergent Feelings Between Group Members
ST	Structuring
FC	Forcing a Member to Develop a Topic
DQ	Direct Question to a Member or Group as Whole
FD	Friendly Discussion
HU	Humor
UC	Unclassifiable
PA	Pause
CQ	Clarifying Question
ND	Nondirective Lead
GI	Giving Information
SS	Summarizing Statement

Note: These categories were not ranked.

Although previous investigators have used but one category for clarification of feeling, it will be noted in Table 7 that eight subdivisions of this category are employed in the present research. This was done to establish finer definitions of this particular type of group leader behavior. The clinical experience of the investigators led them to believe that certain types of clarification of feeling were followed by unfavorable client reactions. Therefore, these additional categories made it possible to test hypotheses which would either tend to confirm or question this clinical observation. Wherever it proved impossible to judge the direction and quality of the feeling expressed by a group member, the group leader response to that member was scored with the more general category CF.

Further examination of Table 7 reveals that categories of group leader behavior, such as advice, suggestion, persuasion, interpretation, and reassurance, are not listed. Other studies in nondirective therapy have included such categories, but the group leaders in this study did not use them at all and consequently they are not included in this table.

The Problem of Evaluating the Initial Personal Adjustment of Group Members

An evaluation of the initial personal adjustment of all the group members was another crucial problem in this research, for many hypotheses are developed which use this estimate as a criterion of initial classification.

It was at once apparent that it would be rather indefensible to state health or adjustment in a quantity or score. Instead, it was considered feasible and justifiable to rank the group members among themselves, assigning them relative positions on a continuum proceeding from good to poor adjustment. If the seventeen members could be ranked for adjustment by the three group leaders who knew them clinically, intimately, and intensively by virtue of therapy contacts and if this ranking were significantly correlated with an independent measure, the correlation coefficient would test the validity of that ranking.

In a round-table discussion among the three researchers (the group leaders) who had prepared short essays on their clinical evaluation of each individual's adjustment, a ranking of initial health for the seventeen individuals was agreed upon. This ranking was based merely upon clinical evidence and was uncontaminated by knowledge of the Rorschachs which were to serve as the independent measures. The latter had been administered by the researchers six months prior to the clinical judgments but they remained cabinet-filed and unscored.

The Rorschachs were scored after the clinical ranking had been determined in the manner described above and sixteen psychograms (one member had not received a Rorschach) were prepared on standard Klopfer-Davidson Individual Record Blanks. These tabulations were submitted to three competent Rorschach workers, who were asked to rank the records for personal adjustment. Rorschach protocol data were not submitted for judging. These three rankings were then correlated with the clinical rankings of adjustment; the coefficients are given in Table 8.

TABLE 8. RANK ORDER CORRELATION COEFFICIENTS BETWEEN CLINICAL
RANKING OF PRE-THERAPY ADJUSTMENT OF 16 GROUP MEMBERS
AND RANKING OF THEIR PRE-THERAPY RORSCHACH
PSYCHOGRAMS BY THREE JUDGES

	Judge I	Judge II	Judge III	Clinical Ranking
Judge I	—	.71	.75	.79
Judge II		—	.89	.83
Judge III			—	.80
Clinical Ranking				—

The values of the correlation coefficients tend to lend validity to the clinical ranking of adjustment. Although the validity of the ranking was studied in sixteen cases (one member had not received a Rorschach), the ranking of seventeen members prepared from clinical observation was preserved for use when it was required in testing hypotheses.

*The Problem of Deriving Groups of Most-Profited
and Least-Profited Members*

The investigation was faced with the necessity of deriving a measure of therapeutic gain for use as a method of classification in subjecting hypotheses to verification. It was considered rather difficult to justify ranking members for amount of therapeutic gain although this method would have resulted in finer discriminations when hypotheses were tested. The cooperating researchers concluded that the most justifiable procedure would be the separation of the sixteen group members (one member had withdrawn from therapy) into two smaller groups—one to represent the members who profited most from the group psychotherapy experience and the other to represent those members who profited little or not at all.

Again several measures were available for use in arriving at this grouping. It was felt that the pre- and post-tests might provide some index of therapeutic profit and that they might be used to give validity to clinical judgments of gain by the group leaders.

Proceeding in this manner, the three group leaders made judgments of "profit" or "little-profit" for each of the sixteen group members. This was based upon clinical observation of change and reports about life experiences which the group leaders evaluated from their own clinical experience. These judgments were then checked for agreement with the instruments which had been administered before and immediately after the group therapy. The tests, available for examination, were an Incomplete-Sentences Test, a Self-Rating Checklist, and the Rorschach. Since the Rorschach may be describing a basic personality structure which might be intractable to short-term psychotherapy and since the literature [56, 14] reports conflicting results in its use as an instrument to measure therapeutic gain, it was abandoned in favor of the other two tests.

The other instruments (the Incomplete-Sentences Test and the Self-Rating Checklist) were scored by comparing each item of the individual's first test record with the corresponding item of his second. A healthier "response-difference" was scored plus (+), while a less healthy "response-difference" was scored minus (−). Instances of no apparent difference were scored zero (0). When the algebraic sums for each pair of tests were computed, those individuals on the plus side were considered improved, while those scoring zero or minus were considered as not improved.

TABLE 9. PERCENT OF AGREEMENT BETWEEN CLINICAL JUDGMENT OF DEGREE OF GAIN AND PRE- AND POST-THERAPY TEST SCORE DIFFERENCES

	Percent
Clinical Judgment, Incomplete-Sentences Test	75
Clinical Judgment, Self-Rating Checklist	81
Incomplete-Sentences Test, Self-Rating Checklist	81

The agreement of the tests with the clinical judgments of the group leaders were calculated, and Table 9 gives the values. Agreement is sufficiently high to suggest that the judgments are possessed of some validity and those judgments were preserved for use.

It was now possible to proceed to the testing of the research hypotheses. A suitable and reliable method for quantifying verbatim group therapy protocols had been devised, and judgments with reference to initial member adjustment and gain from psychotherapy were apparently of some validity.[1]

---

[1] The use of more appropriate statistical method in some few instances has here yielded conclusions at variance with some of the conclusions reported in the original doctoral theses (on file in Teachers College Library).

CHAPTER IV

THE NATURE OF THE GROUP PROCESS IN NONDIRECTIVE GROUP PSYCHOTHERAPY

Erasmus L. Hoch

Analysis of the data proceeded with a twofold aim. Its basic purpose was to ascertain whether there is indeed something to which we can refer as the characteristic nondirective group psychotherapy process. If this assumption seemed justified, there remained the additional task of defining the nature of this process with respect to specified variables.

The largely speculative nature of the literature in the field left no dearth of reasonable hypotheses to be tested. In order that the research should not grow to unmanageable proportions, however, the choice of questions selected for investigation had of necessity to be limited. While decision on the hypotheses to be tested was therefore somewhat arbitrary, it was governed by such considerations as the generalized significance of a hypothesis, its appropriateness from the standpoint of experimental design, the relevance of its implications, and similar features.

As a consequence of this process of delimitation, there were singled out what seemed to be three fundamental questions. At the same time, under each of these were subsumed specific subquestions which appeared both to grow out of them and to contribute to their completeness. By way of making more intelligible the analysis of the data which follows, these propositions, together with their subpropositions, are listed here.

I. There is a characteristic nondirective group psychotherapy process.
   A. This process is sufficiently similar from group to group to be regarded as a typical process.

    B. This process exhibits typical trends which can be charted.

    C. Temporal cross sections of this process are significantly different from one another.

II. There are characteristic nondirective group psychotherapy subprocesses.

    A. Although the process of one group is highly similar to that of another group, within each group the processes of the respective individual members vary considerably among themselves.

    B. These member subprocesses differ from one another principally in terms of the variable of gain.

III. Process phenomena are definable as functions of specifiable variables.

    A. "Discord" is a function of specifiable variables.

    B. "Gain" is a function of specifiable variables.

The rationale which underlies this particular selection and arrangement of propositions is that of analyzing the findings in terms of progressively increasing specificity. Proposition I concerns itself with the broadest aspects of the process, the similarity of groups as groups. A closer view of this process is sought in Proposition II, which analyzes its subprocesses. Finally, Proposition III attempts to examine the core of the process by its efforts at internal analysis.

ANALYSIS OF THE GROUP PROCESS

The Degree of Intergroup Similarity

It was hypothesized from the outset that the process being studied was one which could be considered the characteristic nondirective group psychotherapy process. That is, it was expected that the verbal behavior of members as a group could be shown to be sufficiently similar from group to group to warrant its being regarded as the typical process occurring in this type of therapy. In order to investigate this question it was necessary to devise a method whereby the verbal behavior of the three groups, as groups, could be compared. By virtue of the manner in which the protocols had been analyzed, such a basis for comparison was conveniently available in the form of category frequencies. The distribution of these frequencies represented both the quality and the quantity of the verbal behavior which had taken place. Comparison of these distributions constituted a problem, however. On the one hand, a rank order correlation of the frequencies in the forty-eight categories would have spread the behavior too thinly, that is, several of the categories would have contained rather small frequencies. On the other hand, making comparisons solely in terms of the distribution of frequencies with respect to total "client," total "member-therapist," and total "general" categories employed by the respective groups would have constituted too gross a contrast. At the same time, however, it was apparent that the list of categories[1] could be conveniently grouped in certain natural subdivisions. Thus, for example, client categories C9, C10, and C11 all represented "acceptance" of another individual's remarks, while client categories C15, C16, and C17 represented "rejection" of such remarks. Employing what seemed to constitute natural cut-off points, the forty-eight categories were thereby divided into the following seventeen category groupings:

C1–6, 7–8, 9–11, 12–17, 18–20, 21–22
T1–9, 10, 10W, 11–13, 14, 15–16
G1–3, 4–6, 6W, 7, 8

The frequencies for each such grouping were subsequently tallied for the total therapy cycles of Group A, Group B, and Group C. Ranking the frequencies in these category groupings, the rank order intercorrelations obtained for the three therapy groups were found to be those listed in Table 10.

It will be noted that these intercorrelations are remarkably similar. It was felt immediately, therefore, that this similarity might well be an artifact of the category groupings employed in calculating the intercorrelations, and that any intercorrelations computed in this manner would of necessity be as close. However, as will be shown in a later section, the intercorrelations of the

[1] The present investigation arbitrarily denotes the unit of measurement as all that is contained in an uninterrupted flow of verbal material by a group member. Obviously this procedure involves the use of unequal units and treats them additively. While this is apparently a serious limitation, justification for the procedure is found in the many researches in psychotherapy where utilization of unequal units has yielded generalizations consistent with theoretical views [17, 78, 88].

TABLE 10. RANK ORDER CORRELATIONS FOR THE 17 CATEGORY GROUPINGS RANKED AS TO FREQUENCY OF OCCURRENCE DURING ENTIRE THERAPY CYCLE OF GROUPS A, B, AND C

	Group A	Group B	Group C
Group A	—	.85	.84
Group B		—	.86
Group C			—

category distributions of the individual members—using the same seventeen groupings—exhibit a considerable range. There remained, however, the question of whether the close intergroup similarities were not attributable to the fact that the respective member behaviors canceled each other out—that within each group one member's high frequency in a category grouping was offset by another member's low frequency, yielding an over-all intergroup similarity. While this is undoubtedly the case, it does not alter the fact that, taken as a group, the members in Groups A, B, and C spent their respective sessions in very similar atmospheres with respect to the verbal behavior taking place. That is, regardless of the specific behavior exhibited by any one member in any group, the verbal environment in which he spent his time over the course of the therapy cycle was similar to the climate which existed for other members in other groups. The evidence, therefore, points in the direction of a standard, typical experience which a participant in nondirective group psychotherapy may reasonably be expected to undergo—the experience of working through his problems in a definable, characteristic verbal atmosphere.

A general view of the more prominent features of such an experience may be gained by examining the higher-rank category groupings in the three groups. Thus, for example, using ranks 1 to 7, one finds that the same seven types of verbal activity take place in each group more often than the remaining kinds of behavior. These groupings, consisting of three client categories, three member-therapist categories, and one general category, are shown below.

TABLE 11. SEVEN MOST FREQUENTLY OCCURRING TYPES OF VERBAL BEHAVIOR IN GROUPS A, B, AND C

C7–8	T1–9	G4–6
C9–11	T10	
C18–20	T11–13	

Taking these seven most frequently displayed types of activity and calculating the mean rank of each, one finds that they occur in the order indicated in Table 12.

TABLE 12. MEAN RANKS OF SEVEN MOST FREQUENTLY OCCURRING TYPES OF VERBAL BEHAVIOR IN GROUPS A, B, AND C

Behavior Category Grouping	Mean Rank
G4–6	1
T11–13	2.7
C7–8	3
C9–11	3.7
T1–9	5.7
C18–20	5.7
T10	6.3

Examination of these ranks discloses the fact that the type of behavior which led all others was an intellectual kind of problem discussion, that is, more often than they did anything else, the members interacted with one another and their problems in a minimally ego-involving fashion. This finding is especially worth noting in view of the failure of the literature to point up the extreme prominence of this type of activity in group therapy. The fact that the group members were graduate students may, however, have some bearing in this connection.

While such a finding may tend to convey the impression that much of what took place was of an impersonal nature, this notion is corrected when the successively higher ranks are examined. Only in seventh place does one find the next type of activity which might be so construed—T10 ("Expression of Opinion")—and even this constitutes an intended therapeutic helpfulness on the part of one member in relation to another. In the intervening ranks is found behavior of a substantially therapeutic nature according to generally accepted criteria. Thus, second most frequent (T11–13) is the effort on the part of one member to be of aid to another either by requesting him to elaborate upon his problem, or by advising him concerning it, or by interpreting to him its nature. Almost as frequent is the related attempt by a member to specify his problems and to elaborate upon them (C7–8). That this type of mutual assistance was generally conceived by the respective members as well-intentioned is evidenced by the fact that in fourth place appears the tendency to accept whatever clarifications, opinions, or interpretations were proffered (C9–11).

Occurring next most often on the average are two types of behavior which similarly exemplify the dual motivation of members with respect to getting and giving help. On the one hand is manifested the desire of a member to bring order out of his chaos while he is not yet free enough to dispense with defensiveness and evasion (C18–20). Counteracting this are the overt evidences on the part of other members to understand, sympathize with, and encourage whoever in the group seems at the time to require such assistance (T1–9).

Although it would be possible to rank similarly the remaining categories, the ones noted convey in some degree the flavor of the nondirective group psychotherapy experience. Its fuller depiction, it is felt, is more expeditiously furthered by the types of analysis which follow.

Typical Group Process Trends

On the basis of the results obtained by investigators of the individual nondirective psychotherapy process, it was reasonable to hypothesize that certain functions would rise and others fall in the course of the group therapy cycle. It was assumed, for example, that with successive sessions the more positive verbal behavior would increase in frequency, the more negative verbal behavior decrease.

In investigating this aspect of the problem the frequencies for the cycles of each group as a whole were plotted with respect to the three functions which have received widest attention in the literature—expression of positive emotion, expression of negative emotion, and problem discussion.[2] On this basis, a charting of the expression of positive emotion as a function of time—using categories C1 through C6 as indices—yielded the graphs shown in Figure 1. It is apparent that the slope of a best-fitting straight line would be significantly different from that of a line whose slope is zero.

[2] Since Gorlow's section of the study was concerned specifically with members' "therapist" behavior, the present investigator restricted his efforts to charting "client" behavior.

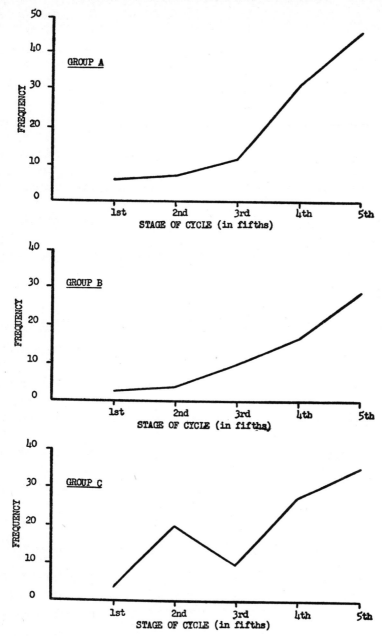

FIGURE 1. DISTRIBUTION OF POSITIVE CLIENT BEHAVIOR IN THE COURSE
OF THERAPY CYCLES OF GROUPS A, B, AND C, CATEGORIES C1–C6

As will be noted, in the cycle of each of the groups the expression of positive emotion follows a generally rising course. This marked increase in the frequency of behavior of a positive type becomes the more pronounced when contrasted with the expression of negative emotion as a function of time. The latter, similarly charted, appears in Figure 2, categories C21 and C22 serving as the corresponding indices.

On the basis of the findings in individual psychotherapy investigations, it had been hypothesized that the graph of negative emotion would be the reverse of that of positive emotion, that is, the expression of negative emotion would exhibit a high incidence in initial stages of therapy and a consistent decline as therapy progressed. The findings on this score are somewhat at variance with expectation. In place of the anticipated high initial frequency is found almost an absence of this type of verbal behavior. Only after several sessions does it become at all pronounced, requiring even then almost half the total sessions to reach its peak and start a downward trend.

It would seem plausible to advance the following rationale as underlying this finding. In individual psychotherapy the client makes whatever painful revelations he must to one other person, an individual who already has set the stage for just such disclosures. The group psychotherapy situation, however, contains additional elements (in the form of other clients) which introduce not only quantitative but indeed qualitative differences. While, therefore, in individual therapy a client evidently feels reasonably free from the very beginning to express considerable negative emotion, the findings would indicate that in group therapy there exists a prerequisite "warming-up" period in which members feel each other out, assess each other's personality attributes, and cautiously test the limits of the situation. This very feature of group therapy is, in fact, hinted at in the literature. White [99], for example, in enumerating the successive stages through which the therapy process passes, lists as the first a "party behavior" period. Apparently only after this phase has been passed is there a general readiness on the part of the group to give vent, with genuine spontaneity, to feelings not customarily regarded as "nice." Thereafter the expression of negative emotion proceeds with considerable freedom to a

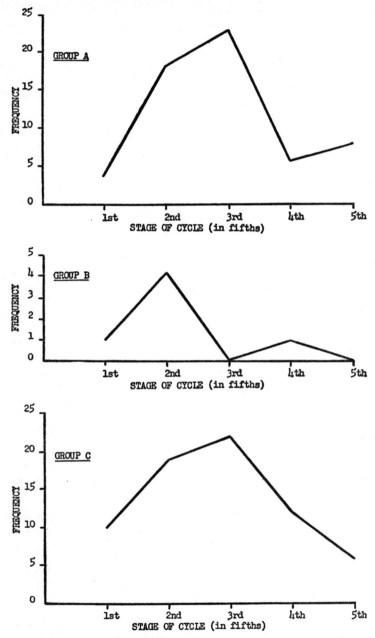

FIGURE 2. DISTRIBUTION OF NEGATIVE CLIENT BEHAVIOR IN THE COURSE OF THERAPY CYCLES OF GROUPS A, B, AND C, CATEGORIES C21–C22

point at which positive gain factors are evidently assuming the upper hand, allowing negative feelings to bow out in deference to the former.

With reference to problem-stating activity—as defined by categories C7 and C8—individual psychotherapy findings had led to the expectation that this type of behavior would occur with considerable frequency in the early stages of group therapy and then decline consistently almost to the vanishing point. Plotting the incidence of this activity as a function of time yielded the graphs shown in Figure 3.

The graph of this function serves to point up a phenomenon which apparently characterizes the group situation, namely, that problem-stating is present in considerable force even at the conclusion of therapy. It is conceivable that this finding in the present instance is to be attributed to the somewhat arbitrary termination of the therapy cycles by the mid-term disruption of members' time schedules. A closer examination of the nature of the problems stated in the course of the process points, however, to another explanation, which has three features. In the first place, members apparently choose to "make the rounds" with respect to stating problems, taking turns at serving as central figure. Secondly, it is discovered that as a rule the original presenting problem is the first chosen by a given member for group presentation. Finally, the rounds of problem-stating seem to take place at successively deeper levels, many members revealing their "real problem" as late as the second half of therapy, apparently when they feel completely confident of their acceptance. This phenomenon, it is felt, underlies the fluctuations exhibited by the curve of this function.

On the basis of intergroup similarities, therefore, it would seem justifiable to conclude that in group psychotherapy, as in individual psychotherapy, certain types of verbal behavior exhibit characteristic progressions as a function of time. As in individual psychotherapy, the expression of positive emotion shows a rather consistently rising trend in the course of the group therapy cycle; the expression of negative emotion requires a period manifestly devoted to the gaining of confidence in the other members before making its appearance, and once having done so, rising to a peak in the middle of therapy and declining from that point on; prob-

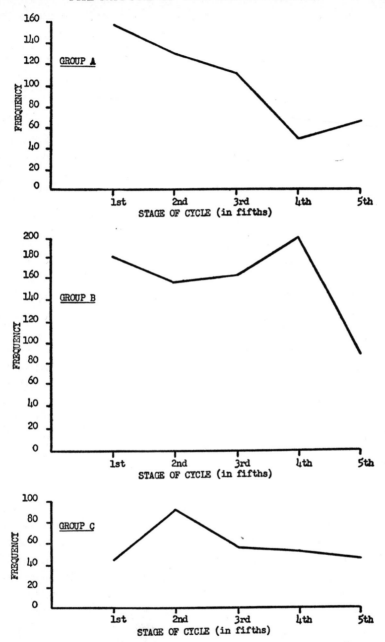

FIGURE 3. DISTRIBUTION OF PROBLEM-STATING BEHAVIOR IN THE COURSE OF THERAPY CYCLES OF GROUPS A, B, AND C, CATEGORIES C7–C8

lem-stating activity shows no clear-cut pattern, exhibiting, however, the tendency to be present in considerable force even at the conclusion of therapy, the problems brought forth being at that period on a deeper level than those initially posed.

Temporal Cross Sections of the Group Process—
Null Hypothesis

There is no significant difference in the quality of the verbal behavior taking place during the first and second halves of the therapy cycle.

It was expected that during the second half of the therapy cycle members would behave verbally in a more therapeutic manner than they had during the first. In order to test this hypothesis, the cycle of each group was divided into two halves on the basis of the number of sessions it had met. Next, the categories of verbal behavior were classified into two types—best categories (most therapeutic) and poorest categories (least therapeutic). It was decided at the outset that client categories C1 ("Discussion of Plans") through C6 ("Ambivalent Acceptance of Others") and member-therapist categories T1 ("Clarification of Feeling") through T9 ("Reassurance") would serve as the best categories, while client categories C18 ("Confusion") through C22 ("Negative Attitude Toward Self") and member-therapist categories T15 ("Evaluation") through T16 ("Disapproval") would represent the poorest categories of verbal behavior.

When the hypothesis tested is that the population mean difference (in group members' use of categories C1 through C6 in the first and second halves of therapy) is zero, a value of $t = 4.51$ is obtained for the sample mean difference of 9.25. When this value is referred to Student's distribution for 15 degrees of freedom, the conclusion is that a value of t as large as or larger than this would occur through the accidents of sampling in less than 2 per 100 samples from the hypothetical population. The hypothesis that the mean difference is zero may therefore be rejected and the conclusion drawn that client behavior of a positive nature is significantly more in evidence during the second half of therapy.

When, on the other hand, the hypothesis is tested that the population mean difference (in group members' use of categories C18 through C22 in the first and second halves of therapy) is zero, a value of $t = 1.23$ is obtained for the sample mean difference of 7.12. Since a value as large as this or larger could be obtained in more than 20 per 100 samples purely through the accidents of sampling, the hypothesis that the mean difference is zero cannot be rejected. Although client behavior of a distinctly negative kind does decline appreciably in the second half of therapy, it does not do so to a degree which can be termed statistically significant.

A similar analysis of the data with respect to best and poorest member-therapist categories yielded in each instance statistically significant differences between members' use of such categories between the first and second halves of therapy. The results are reported in Gorlow's section of the study.

Summarizing the findings up to this point, then, one notes the following. The three nondirective psychotherapy groups studied resembled each other considerably in terms of the verbal behavior exhibited. Trends which typify this behavior appeared to be similar in the three groups, and, in terms of time, cross sections of the process were in several important respects significantly different from each other with respect to the quality of the verbal behavior taking place. Admittedly the methodological limitations of the present study do not permit generalizations from the three groups to all nondirective psychotherapy groups. However, the results, taken collectively, suggest that speculation as to the existence of a characteristic nondirective group psychotherapy process may be a fruitful lead in future research.

ANALYSIS OF THE GROUP SUBPROCESSES

The type of theorizing out of which had grown the preceding hypothesis gave rise to further analogous assumptions with respect to the components of the group therapy process. In accordance with the generally accepted principles of Gestalt psychology, it was anticipated that the whole—the process of the group in aggregate— and its parts—the respective processes of the individual members —would be found to stand in certain relationships to each other.

Two subhypotheses consequently emerged. First, it was expected that if the group process represented not a summation but rather an integration of its individual member processes, intragroup differences might be pronounced and yet not affect the essential similarity of total group processes. Secondly, it was felt that if one sought some criterion for classifying the subprocesses, the variable of gain would constitute the most probable distinguishing factor.

The Degree of Intragroup Similarity

The group process intercorrelations reported under Hypothesis I indicate that in the course of a nondirective group therapy experience the members operate in a characteristic, definable verbal climate. Although it had been hypothesized that the group process as such would follow this typical, predictable course, it had been anticipated that the subprocesses within this total group process would exhibit individual differences.

TABLE 13. INTERCORRELATIONS OF FREQUENCIES IN MEMBERS' CATEGORY DISTRIBUTIONS IN GROUPS A, B, AND C

Group A

	Member No. 1	Member No. 2	Member No. 3	Member No. 4	Member No. 5	Member No. 6
Member No. 1	—	.52	.58	.93	.92	.78
Member No. 2		—	.88	.46	.75	.83
Member No. 3			—	.61	.81	.86
Member No. 4				—	.86	.81
Member No. 5					—	.88
Member No. 6						—

Group B

	Member No. 1	Member No. 2	Member No. 3	Member No. 4	Member No. 5
Member No. 1	—	.84	.95	.97	.94
Member No. 2		—	.81	.85	.87
Member No. 3			—	.91	.83
Member No. 4				—	.91
Member No. 5					—

Group C

	Member No. 1	Member No. 2	Member No. 3	Member No. 4	Member No. 5	Member No. 6
Member No. 1	—	.54	.75	.77	.71	.60
Member No. 2		—	.64	.52	.58	.84
Member No. 3			—	.57	.72	.61
Member No. 4				—	.82	.56
Member No. 5					—	.60
Member No. 6						—

Using the procedure employed in calculating the intergroup correlations, intercorrelations were similarly computed between the category distributions of the respective members within each group. The results appear in Table 13 above.

Unlike the close similarity existing among groups collectively, the intermember correlations, as can be seen from Table 13, display a considerable range. On the one hand, this bears out the conviction that the whole is greater than the sum of its parts in the sense that the complexion of group behavior is multi-determined rather than conditioned upon the activity of any given member. On the other hand, it indicates the autonomy which characterizes each part within a whole, since despite the high intergroup correlations, individual member behaviors do not allow themselves to be cast in a uniform mold.

The Verbal Behavior of Most-Profited and Least-Profited Members—Null Hypothesis

There is no significant qualitative difference between the verbal behavior of most-profited members and that of least-profited members.

It was expected that if the processes of members considered to have profited most from the therapy experience were compared with those judged to have profited least, a significant difference would be revealed. Employing the same group of categories defined under Hypothesis I as "best" and "poorest," the individual processes of the eight most-profited members were compared with those of the eight least-profited. (Since one member—in the least-profited group—had been present for only twelve of the nineteen sessions of his group, his category frequencies were omitted from this calculation.)

As reported in Gorlow's section of the study, a comparison of the member-therapist behavior of most-profited and least-profited members reveals significant differences in their respective use of "best" as contrasted with "poorest" therapist categories.

The present investigator was concerned primarily with the use of client categories by most-profited and least-profited members in the course of the therapy cycle. It was expected that in this mode of behavior, too, those who gained most from the experience and those who gained least would likewise reveal significant differences.

In order to test this hypothesis, the client behavior of most-profited members in the first half of therapy was compared with their client behavior in the second half with respect to their use of "best" client categories (C1 through C6) as previously defined; their use of "poorest" client categories (C18 through C22) was similarly compared. An identical type of analysis was likewise performed with respect to least-profited members.

When the most-profited members' use of "best" client categories (C1 through C6) in the first half of therapy is compared with their use in the second half, a value of $t = 3.18$ is obtained for the sample mean difference of 8.6. A similar comparison in the case of least-profited members yields a value of $t = 3.92$ for the sample mean difference of 9.8. At 7 degrees of freedom a value as large as or larger than either of these would occur through the accidents of sampling in less than 2 per 100 samples from the hypothetical population. Since both most-profited and least-profited members, therefore, employ significantly more therapeutic client behavior in the second half of therapy, this mode of behavior does not afford a basis for distinguishing one group from the other.

When, however, "poorest" client behavior (client categories C18 through C22) during the first and second halves of therapy is compared, significant differences are revealed between most-profited and least-profited members. Comparing most-profited members' use of categories C18 through C22 in the first and second halves of therapy yields a value of $t = 2.72$ for the sample mean difference of 10.6. At 7 degrees of freedom a value as large as or larger than this would occur through the accidents of sampling in less than 5 per 100 samples from the hypothetical population. On the other hand, when least-profited members' use of categories C18 through C22 in the first and second halves of therapy is compared, a value of $t = .32$ is obtained for the sample mean difference of 3.6. A value so small could easily have been obtained through the accidents of sampling.

A convenient basis for distinguishing the behavior of most-profited and least-profited members thus suggests itself. While the former group employs significantly less client behavior of the less therapeutic kind (categories C18 through C22) in the latter half of therapy, the least-profited members fail to change their behavior significantly in this respect. Taken together, the results imply that most-profited and least-profited members tend to look upon both themselves and others more favorably as a consequence of the therapeutic experience, but that least-profited members still retain considerable of their negative views, whereas most-profited members slough these off significantly.

It was felt further that there would be found a significant difference not only between the ratios in which better and poorer categories were used but even with respect to the percentage of responses falling within the three broad groups—client, member-therapist, and general categories. These percentages were therefore calculated for each member by dividing the number of his client, member-therapist, and general categories respectively by his total categories, yielding for each participant a Client %, a Therapist %, and a General %. These percentages are shown in Table 14.

TABLE 14. PERCENT OF EACH MEMBER'S TOTAL RESPONSES FALLING IN CLIENT, MEMBER-THERAPIST, AND GENERAL CATEGORIES

CLIENT CATEGORIES		THERAPIST CATEGORIES		GENERAL CATEGORIES	
Most-profited Members	Least-profited Members	Most-profited Members	Least-profited Members	Most-profited Members	Least-profited Members
%	%	%	%	%	%
61	69	58	38	35	50
60	53	55	35	34	41
58	45	55	32	34	39
43	44	33	30	28	37
33	44	22	29	23	35
26	42	18	15	22	34
23	35	16	13	22	24
14	34	8	10	19	21
	23		8		20
Mean					
40	43	33	23	27	34

While the respective means (shown in the last row of Table 14) point up certain differences, a *t*-test of the significance of these differences yields *t* values not conclusive for client, therapist, and general categories respectively, none of them being significant at the 5 percent level. While, therefore, most-profited members differed significantly from least-profited members with respect to quality of categories employed, no real difference has been demonstrated with respect to the frequency of their use of client, therapist, and general types of categories as such. In terms of the obtained means, least-profited members exceed most-profited members in the use of client and general categories, while most-profited members exceed least-profited members in the use of therapist categories. Although the test of significance indicates that these differences may not justifiably be regarded as genuine, the figures themselves point up the necessity for more intensive investigation of two possibilities: (a) that gain in group therapy derives not only from being acted upon by others, but also from acting upon them; (b) that most-profited members spend a larger share of their time than do least-profited members in ego-involving behavior as compared with intellectual discourse.

With respect to the hypothesis that there exist characteristic subprocesses in nondirective group psychotherapy, the following may therefore be concluded. First, while nondirective therapy groups, as groups, show a marked similarity in the type of behavior in which they engage, the members, among themselves, display a considerable diversity of verbal activity. Secondly, a serviceable criterion for differentiating and classifying member subprocesses is the variable of derived gain, which reveals significant differences between the quality of verbal categories employed by those who gain most and least from the therapy experience.

ANALYSIS OF PROCESS PHENOMENA

In accounting for the phenomena which characterize the group psychotherapy process, there is in the literature a general tendency to invoke standard psychoanalytic concepts. It seemed to the present investigators, therefore, quite worth while to examine the question of whether it is possible to define such phenomena as functions of specifiable variables without introducing extraneous symbolic constructs. Two such phenomena—each of which has been the focus of considerable attention in the literature—will be considered. In each instance, of course, no claim is made to an exhaustive analysis of the phenomenon in question. Rather, the intent is suggestive in nature.

"Discord" as a Function of Specifiable Variables

It is possible to view, as most writers in the field do, the verbal friction which occurs in the process of group therapy as a vying for the affection of a parent (the group therapist) on the part of his children (the group members), and to dispose of instances of such inter-member wrangling with the explanation that they symbolize the reinstitution of analogous earlier contests for parental affection among children in a family. It is, however, also possible—without introducing symbolic concepts—to ascertain the degree of relationship between such inter-member behavior and certain conditions obtaining at the time of its occurrence.

With reference to this latter point, two initial assumptions had been made by the present investigator. Regarding "sibling rivalry" essentially as "discord," it was felt on the one hand that such discordant behavior would be less in evidence when there was being discussed a topic with respect to which most of the members could experience a certain empathy. Secondly, it was conjectured that the greater the similarity of the verbal behavior patterns of the group members, the less the discord that would arise, while the greater the divergence of their patterns, the more the discord that might be expected.

Null Hypothesis

Between themes having one or no client and themes having several clients there is no significant difference with respect to the degree of discord evident.

In order to test this hypothesis, it was necessary to establish by prearrangement which categories would serve as indices of discord. On the basis of a review of the combined list, nine categories were selected as representing evidences of defensive or discordant behavior on the part of the group members. These categories, constituting samples of client, member-therapist, and general behavior, were: C15, C16, C17, C19, C20, T10W, T15, T16, G6W. Tallying the frequencies in these categories for each theme and dividing these by the total of all categories in that theme yielded a "percent of discord" for each theme of each session in each group.

With such a measure of discordant behavior available, it was possible to test the hypothesis that this discord percentage would be higher for those themes in which the topic of discussion appealed to only one or no members and lower in those themes in which the topic was more general in its appeal. It was decided that the degree of empathy experienced by a member with respect to a given theme would be represented by the fact of whether or not he became a client or a secondary client within that theme. That is, it was assumed that those themes in which a given member served as client or secondary client represented for him pertinent areas of discussion, while those in which he did not assume the role of client constituted themes in which he felt less personal involvement. On this basis the themes within each group's total cycle were divided into two groups—those which had more than one client and those which had one or no client. (A theme was considered as having no client when the verbal behavior within it fell essentially into "general" categories.) At the same time, the themes within each group's cycle were ranked in terms of the percent of discord previously described—a rank of 1 being assigned the most discordant theme. Using the middle rank as a dividing point, and dividing the themes of each group into ranks higher and lower than this midpoint, this percentage of discord was examined for its relationship to the number of clients in the respective themes. The resultant chi-squares are shown in Table 15.

The statistical evidence in this case is somewhat inconclusive. While the chi-squares for Groups A and B are significant at the 1 percent level, that for Group C is not. It is reasonable to assume, therefore, that factors in addition to the one here considered determine the degree of discordant behavior in a theme. One such other possible factor—that hypothesized previously, namely the degree of similarity between members' verbal behavior patterns—was consequently examined. An index of the degree to which members approximated one another's use of categories in terms of both quantity and quality was already available in the form of the intercorrelations of their category frequency distributions listed in Table 13 under Hypothesis II. It was felt that the dispersion of these intercorrelations within a group would constitute a measure of the general degree of similarity obtaining between the

TABLE 15. RELATIONSHIP BETWEEN PERCENT OF DISCORD RANKINGS OF THEMES AND NUMBERS OF CLIENTS IN RESPECTIVE THEMES

Group A

	Rank above 25	Rank below 25
Themes with one or no client	22	12
Themes with more than one client	2	13

Chi-square† 9.02** at 1 d.f.

Group B

	Rank above 23	Rank below 23
Themes with one or no client	14	3
Themes with more than one client	9	19

Chi-square† 8.75** at 1 d.f.

Group C

	Rank above 15.5	Rank below 15.5
Themes with one or no client	11	7
Themes with more than one client	4	8

Chi-square† 1.25

†Chi-square adjusted by Yates's correction (for small cell frequencies).

respective behavior patterns. The standard deviation of these intercorrelations was consequently computed for each group. At the same time, a "group percent of discord" was calculated for the respective groups by dividing the total discordant frequencies (as previously defined) by the total group frequencies. The relationships found between these two factors are indicated in Table 16.

TABLE 16. RELATIONSHIP BETWEEN INTERMEMBER SIMILARITY OF BEHAVIOR PATTERNS AND PERCENT OF GROUP DISCORD

	Group Discord Percent	Standard Deviation of Intermember Correlations Within the Group
Group B	3.6	.05
Group C	10.4	.10
Group A	12.5	.14

Although the statistical procedure employed in Table 16 is not definitive, it would suggest tentatively that the more varied the verbal behavior patterns employed by the members of a group, the greater the expected friction among the members.

This examination of the phenomenon of discord in group behavior does not in any sense purport to be conclusive. At the same time, however, it suggests the distinct possibility of explaining certain observed phenomena on the basis of more tangible measures than are generally employed. Only after the relationships existing between such functions and the phenomena in question have been thoroughly investigated would it seem defensible to introduce explanations of a symbolic nature.

"Gain" as a Function of Specifiable Variables

Since the whole concept of group psychotherapy is founded on the premise that individuals can and do gain as the result of such an experience, it is only natural that the literature contain numerous references to this factor. The speculation on this score concerns itself largely with two issues: (*a*) the role which insight into personality difficulties plays in relation to the amount of gain derived; (*b*) the degree of personality reorganization which occurs as a function of gain.

Taking a lead from Hobbs [34], the present investigator conjectured that insight was not the crucial factor in determining gain that it had been made out to be. Turning to a related factor, the degree to which personality structure is altered in connection with gain, it was felt similarly that this had been overrated in the literature. The questions raised were, then, the following. Does insight assume the significance which is customarily ascribed to it? Is there a fundamental reorganization of personality structure as a consequence of gain in group therapy? Since these are issues which *per se* merit intensive investigation, the following findings purport to be merely tentative clues for further research rather than final answers in any sense. (Table 17)

TABLE 17. RELATION OF "INSIGHT" CATEGORY (C2) TO TOTAL CATEGORIES IN THERAPY GROUPS A, B, AND C

	Number of C2 Categories	C2/Total Categories %
Group A	21	0.5
Group B	19	0.6
Group C	22	0.9

One is struck at once by the fact that a type of verbal behavior which is customarily presumed to be so vital should manifest itself so infrequently in the course of the therapy cycle. If one is not to conclude that such verbal activity has been vastly overrated as a concomitant of gain, it is necessary to offer two explanations. Either insight does not bear a one-to-one relation to gain, or else the real nature of insight has eluded us. Further steps were consequently taken to investigate these possibilities.

With respect to the first possibility, the necessary data were already available. On the one hand, it had been decided (as noted in Chapter III) which members had profited most and which least from therapy. On the other, the categories employed by each member during the process had been tallied. It was therefore possible to determine what fraction of each group's total C2 categories—"insight"—had been contributed by the respective members. (Since one member of Group B had left after the twelfth session, leaving only one other least-profited member in that group, only Groups A and C were examined.) Table 18 presents the obtained figures.

TABLE 18. PERCENT OF GROUP'S TOTAL "INSIGHT" CATEGORIES CONTRIBUTED BY MOST-PROFITED AND LEAST-PROFITED MEMBERS IN GROUPS A AND C

	PERCENT CONTRIBUTED BY MEMBERS	
	Most-profited	Least-profited
	%	%
Group A	59	23
	6	12
		0
		0
	65	35
Group C	41	14
	36	9
	0	0
	77	23

Viewing the members as groups, most-profited as against least-profited, it is evident that the former contributed in larger measure to the groups' "insight" category totals. When the figures are examined individually, however, it is noted that in each group some of the least-profited members contributed more to this category than did some of the most-profited. While this statistical analysis is admittedly unrefined, it serves nonetheless to point up the necessity for questioning some rather generally accepted premises.

A recent article by Hobbs [34], who conceives of insight as an "epiphenomenon" rather than the more usual on-the-spot sensing of hitherto unperceived relationships, suggested carrying the process a step further by raising a related question. Is insight really a precursor of change of outlook and behavior (as customarily alleged), or is it rather the verbalization of a change which has already occurred?

Again, data on the basis of which this question could be examined were already available in the form of vebatim responses which had been scored "insight." The latter were subsequently submitted to two qualified judges with instructions independently to decide in as many instances as possible whether the verbalization represented an on-the-spot sensing of previously undetected relationships or whether it constituted the reporting of a change of perspective which had already occurred, that is, an insight-after-the-fact. The judges, whose agreement was 74 percent, subsequently discussed responses on which they had differed and arrived at the final judgments shown in Table 19.

TABLE 19. NATURE OF "INSIGHT" CATEGORIES OF GROUPS A AND C AS DECIDED BY TWO JUDGES

	Group A %	Group C %
Insight-after-the-fact*	67	60
On-the-spot Insight**	19	18
Indeterminate	14	22

* Examples:
   (a) "I, too, have noticed, since I've been coming here, that that is what I have been doing all of my life."
   (b) "And I realized that that too was due to the way I looked."
** Examples:
   (a) "I just realized now what you said."
   (b) (Pause) "I wonder if mother really feels that way or if she's just using that."

It must be admitted that this examination of the issue is hardly adequate. Certainly, however, the nature of these tentative findings calls into question generally held concepts of the nature and function of the phenomenon of insight and emphasizes the need for intensive investigation of its role in therapeutic change.

Turning to the aforementioned second major source of attention in the literature, namely, the degree of personality reorganization involved in gain in therapy, a second hypothesis was framed. It was felt that unless a very intensive form of therapy were employed (and possibly not even under those conditions), the thoroughgoing alteration of character structure which some writers assumed to take place as the result of group psychotherapy was quite improbable. Rather, it was felt that, granted that gain had taken place, a member's personality structure at the conclusion of group psychotherapy would still in large measure reflect his personality structure at its commencement. Couched in these terms, the hypothesis to be tested was the following.

Null Hypothesis

There is no significant relationship between a client's initial verbal behavior and his subsequent verbal behavior throughout the therapy cycle.

To test this hypothesis, the frequency distribution of the categories employed by each member of each group in the first two sessions was arranged in the seventeen category groupings described under Hypothesis I. Similarly, the category frequencies of the member's behavior were tallied under the same seventeen category groupings for the remaining sessions. Ranking the frequency totals in these category groupings for Sessions 1 and 2 as well as those for the remaining sessions, rank order correlation coefficients were calculated between the two sets of rankings for each member. These are reported in Table 20.

The fact that each of these coefficients is significant at the 5 percent level allows rejection of the null hypothesis and permits the conclusion that even a small sample of a member's verbal behavior during the initial stages of therapy bears a significant relationship to his behavior during the remainder of the group therapy process. It must be stated that the lowest correlation coefficient, .55, still leaves much of the variance unaccounted for. It cannot be asserted, therefore, that a knowledge of an individual's behavior in the initial stages of therapy would allow one to predict specifically how he would behave in the course of the process. On the other hand, the fact that each of the correlation coefficients is significant at the 5 percent level would seem to suggest that an individual can vary his behavior only within the specific limits imposed by his

TABLE 20. Rank Order Correlations Between Members' Category Frequencies in Sessions 1 and 2 and Their Category Frequencies in Remaining Sessions of Therapy Cycle of Groups A, B, and C

Member	Group	Correlation Coefficient
1	A	.72
2	A	.72
3	A	.88
4	A	.84
5	A	.94
6	A	.73
7	B	.93
8	B	.78
9	B	.79
10	B	.95
11	B	.81
12	C	.75
13	C	Silent during Sessions 1 & 2
14	C	.55
15	C	.67
16	C	.58
17	C	Absent during Sessions 1 & 2

personality structure. Thus, what one finds in nondirective group psychotherapy is apparently not a "reversal of form," that is, a profound alteration of character structure, but rather a qualitative change of feeling and attitude (as expressed in verbal symbols) within the confines of a given personality. Whether this is equally true of all types of group psychotherapy is a question which can only be settled on the basis of research employing other therapeutic techniques.

Again it must be stressed that this examination of only two aspects of gain does not in any sense claim to be conclusive. As has been stated, such was not the purpose of this investigation. It was oriented rather in the direction of showing that phenomena alleged to occur in the course of therapy can feasibly be studied in terms of definable variables and need not remain in the province of speculation or clinical hunch. The results, therefore, are presented not in the guise of conclusive findings but rather as objectively derived clues to which aspects of group therapy merit restricted and intensive analysis by future investigators.

CHAPTER V

AN ANALYSIS OF THE BEHAVIOR OF MEMBERS AS THERAPISTS

Leon Gorlow

The aim of this aspect of the research was to investigate the phenomenon of member-therapist behavior in nondirective group psychotherapy. Member-therapist behavior is defined as the events which occur when a group member, having sought psychotherapy out of personal need, is discovered assuming the role of therapist for other members in the group experience. Since group members are observed to behave differentially in this respect, the study formulated and tested hypotheses which were considered fruitful in understanding the variable behavior of group members in this respect.

Several broad questions were advanced: (1) Does member-therapist behavior in nondirective group psychotherapy reflect a predictable process? (*a*) Is there a difference in the pattern of member-therapist behavior between the halves of group psychotherapy? (*b*) Are certain personality variables (initial personal adjustment, anxiety, and hostility) associated with the *quantity* and *quality* of member-therapist behavior? and (*c*) Is therapeutic gain a variable associated with the quality of member-therapist behavior? (2) Are the quantity and quality of member-therapist behavior predictable? (3) Do certain dynamics characterize the phenomenon of member-therapist behavior? (*a*) Do personal feelings (liking versus disliking other group members) differentiate the quality of member-therapist behavior? and (*b*) Does the quality of member-therapist behavior differentiate the quality of client behavior?

In general, the hypotheses are derived from the view of personality associated with nondirective psychotherapy. This position, recently stated in organized form by Snygg and Combs [90], has for its central concept the perceiving organism who behaves in accord with his own view of the world. Perception, at any moment in time, is in part determined by the needs of the organism and may not be in accord with the reality of a situation as an external observer may perceive it. It is postulated that behavior is to be understood as deriving from these private perceptions. The implications of the theoretical view for the questions formulated in the present research will be presented as each hypothesis is treated below in the body of the chapter.

The present chapter is separated into three major sections, each representing analyses of data to test the specific hypotheses within the broader questions framed at the outset.

MEMBER-THERAPIST BEHAVIOR AS A PREDICTABLE PROCESS

Several hypotheses relating to the process of member-therapist behavior were advanced. It was considered that significant differences would be observed in the patterns of member-therapist behavior between the first half and the second half of the therapeutic sessions. In addition, it was hypothesized that certain personality variables or attributes of members (initial personal adjustment, anxiety, hostility, and gain from psychotherapy) are associated with the quality of member-therapist activity.

In a sense, one may predict that the pattern of member-therapist behavior would change in the course of psychotherapy in that group members learn to emulate the professional therapist. One should expect that therapeutic behavior reflecting permissiveness and acceptance increases, while therapeutic behavior denoting interpretation, evaluation, and criticism decreases. The professional therapist may create the group climate. On the other hand, it was felt that emulation of the group leader does not completely account for the differences in therapist behavior among members. There is variable behavior beyond what may be explained by recourse to emulation.

Variation among group members with reference to several personality variables may differentiate the therapeutic activity of those members. Initial personal adjustment, anxiety, hostility, and gain from psychotherapy were considered variables bearing upon perception. It was hypothesized that the initially healthier, less anxious, less hostile individual would, as a consequence of his private perceptions, behave with greater personal freedom than the less healthy, more anxious, and more hostile individual. It was felt that greater personal freedom would enable an individual to entertain a wider variety of behavior (therapeutic behavior) and would lend him a desire to get closer to people rather than criticize them. Predictably, behavior reflecting relatively more acceptance and less critical evaluation should be characteristic of the group of individuals possessing greater personal freedom.

Is There a Difference in the Pattern of Member-Therapist Behavior Between the Halves of Group Psychotherapy?

The hypothesis was formulated that significant differences in member-therapist behavior would be observed in the halves of the group psychotherapy process. It was felt that the frequencies of member-therapist behavior in categories indicating accepting, permissive behavior would increase, while the frequencies in categories reflecting negative, evaluative behavior would decrease. One may be testing the contagion of the activity of the professional group leader, for his behavior may be an important factor in determining the climate of the group.

The hypothesis lent itself to test by investigation of the quantity of member-therapist behavior for each individual in certain categories. The entire range of member-therapist categories (T1 through T16) was arbitrarily yet rationally cut at several points on the scale. "Clarification of Feeling" (T1) through "Reassurance" (T9) were considered to reflect member-therapist behavior of the positive variety; "Opinions" (T10) through "Deflection" (T14) were considered to indicate more neutral therapist behavior; and "Evaluation" (T15) through "Disapproval, Criticism" (T16) were defined as denoting member-therapist behavior of a decidedly negative kind. The cycles of psychotherapy were cut into halves, and the frequencies of member-therapist behaviors in the two significant classifications (T1 through T9 and T15 through T16) were determined for both halves of the therapy experience for each of the sixteen individuals (one member's frequencies were omitted because he withdrew from psychotherapy).

When the hypothesis tested is that the population mean difference (in group members' use of T1 through T9 in the first and second halves of psychotherapy) is zero, a value of $t = 2.8$ is observed for the sample mean difference of 8.9. When the value is referred to Student's distribution for 15 degrees of freedom, the conclusion is that so large a value of t would occur through the accidents of sampling in less than 2 per 100 samples from the hypothetical population. The hypothesis that the mean difference is zero is rejected. The difference in group members' use of "Clarification of Feeling" (T1) through "Reassurance" (T9) between the halves of psychotherapy is not to be explained by chance, and the investigator concludes that member-therapist behavior of a distinctly positive kind increases significantly in the second half of therapy. By theoretical consideration the direction of difference was predictable.

On testing the hypothesis that the population mean difference (in group members' use of T15 through T16 in the first and second halves of psychotherapy) is zero, a value of $t = 4.5$ is observed for the sample mean difference of 5.4. When the value is referred to Student's distribution for 15 degrees of freedom, the conclusion is that so large a value of t would occur in accidents of sampling in less than 1 per 100 samples from the hypothetical population. The hypothesis that the mean difference is zero is rejected, and the investigator concludes that member-therapist behavior of a decidedly negative variety ("Evaluation," T15, through "Disapproval, Criticism," T16) decreases significantly in the second half of group psychotherapy. Here, as in the consideration of positive member-therapist behavior, the direction of difference was predictable.

On the basis of these data, the investigator tentatively concludes that the pattern of member-therapist behavior changes significantly between the halves of psychotherapy. The change, in view of its predictability and consistency, is representative of a process of nondirective group psychotherapy. Therapeutic behavior denoting permissiveness and acceptance increases, while therapeutic behavior reflecting evaluation and criticism decreases. One may hypothesize that the climate of therapeutic groups is set, in part, by the behavior of the professional therapist. The study of groups conducted under other approaches to therapy is needed to confirm or refute the hypothesis. For example, does member-therapist behavior in groups conducted within the framework of some psychoanalytic derivative evolve toward increased use of interpretive techniques by members?

In the present study, it was further hypothesized that the process of nondirective group psychotherapy will be characterized by a member-therapist patterning which would reveal an increase in nondirective member-therapist behavior, and a decrease in (a) interpretive, evaluative behavior and (b) behavior reflecting interest in case material per se. While this is predictable from the view that the professional therapist, in part, sets the group climate, Schilder [76] from another frame of reference has also suggested that the interest of member-therapists progresses from case material to interest in the individual.

On the scale of member-therapist behavior, "Clarification of Feeling" (T1), "Restatement of Content" (T2), and "Simple Acceptance" (T3) are the equivalent of nondirective behavior; "Interpretation" (T13), "Deflection" (T14), "Evaluation" (T15), and "Disapproval, Criticism" (T16) are the interpretive, evaluative behavior; and "Opinion" (T10), "Requesting Client to Elaborate" (T11), and "Persuasion, Suggestion, Advice" (T12) can be equated with interest in case material. It was considered that significant changes within these classifications would occur between the first and last quarter of group psychotherapy.

In order to test the hypothesis, the frequencies of member-therapist behavior in the three classifications were determined for the first and last quarter of the group therapy experience. With respect to the mean difference in the use of nondirective member-therapist behavior ("Clarification of Feeling," T1, through "Simple Acceptance," T3), a value of $t = 8.4$ is observed for the sample mean difference of 6.7. The sample mean difference in the use of interpretive, evaluative behavior ("Interpretation," T13, through "Disapproval, Criticism," T16) yielded a value of $t = 5.5$ between the first and last quarters of therapy; and the sample mean difference of 13.9 in the use of behavior reflecting interest in case material *per se* ("Opinion," T10, through "Persuasion, Suggestion, Advice," T12) yielded a value of $t = 4.2$. When all these values are referred to Student's distribution, the conclusion is that such results would occur through the accidents of sampling in less than 1 per 100 samples from the hypothetical population. In all three cases, the hypothesis that the mean difference is zero is rejected. The observation that member-therapist behavior in nondirective group psychotherapy evolves toward a pattern reflecting increased nondirective behavior and decreased interpretive, evaluative, and "interest in case material" behavior is held to be tenable.

Are Certain Personality Variables (Initial Personal Adjustment, Anxiety, and Hostility) Associated with the Quantity and Quality of Member-Therapist Behavior?

Several hypotheses relating to the quantity and quality of member-therapist activity were advanced. Consideration of the problem urged that such personality variables as initial personal adjustment, anxiety, and hostility might bear on therapeutic role-playing in the group psychotherapy experience. More specifically, it was formulated that while the sheer *quantity* of member-therapist role-playing was *not* related to the variables, the *quality* was indeed associated with these very factors. It was postulated that the personality variables of initial personal adjustment, anxiety, and hostility would discriminate among the therapist efforts of the members involved in group psychotherapy.

The specific hypotheses were developed from the theory of personality given earlier (p. 2). The theory would hold the three personality variables as having important consequences for behavior, since perception is viewed as determined, in part, by these personality attributes, and behavior is derived from perception. The less well-adjusted individual possesses less capacity than the healthier individual for viewing himself and his world undistortedly. The anxiety-stricken individual has a constricted perception of his environment, while the hostile person also suffers distorted perception as a result of his intense projections. When translated into member-therapist behavior in group psychotherapy experiences, the hypothesis for testing within the present design is: Initial adjustment, anxiety, and hostility reveal no relationship with the sheer quantity of member-therapist behavior, but they yield a significant association with the quality of that behavior.

Analysis of relationship between quantity of member-therapist behavior and the personality variables

In order to test the hypothesis that there is no relationship between the quantity of member-therapist effort and each of the three variables of initial personal adjustment, anxiety, and hostility, measures of each factor had to be obtained.

A first problem involved deriving scores to represent the quantity of member-therapist behavior for each group member. To preclude the possibility that the obtained score would be a function of the method of measurement, values to denote the quantity of member-therapist participation were sought in several different procedures.

Three methods for deriving scores to represent the quantity of each group member's therapeutic efforts suggested themselves upon examination of the transcribed, categorized, and tallied typescripts. One could summate the "T" (member-therapist) contributions for each individual and then rank the members in order of quantity of participation as derived from this score. (The scores involved can be described by the notation T_i, each representing the sum of "T" contributions by each member, "i".) Another ranking could be derived by computing a percentage score for each subject to represent his part of the total member-therapist effort in his therapy group. (These scores can be noted as T_i/T_g, where T_i is the sum of any individual's therapist behavior and T_g is the sum of the entire group therapist behavior.) Or, one could rank the seventeen members by utilizing another percentage score, viz., one to represent each individual's share of "T" in his own total participation as client, therapist, and general participator. (These can be shorthanded as $T_i/(T_i + C_i + G_i)$.)

Table 21 reports the intercorrelations among rankings of quantity of member-therapist behavior when the three methods for yielding rankings were employed. The correlation coefficients suggest that rankings derived by one method are in high agreement with the rankings achieved by the other methods and that these rankings are not an artifact of one kind of measurement. No apparent differences among the methods are observed, offering justification for the use of any of the techniques as a method of measurement.

TABLE 21.   RANK ORDER CORRELATION COEFFICIENTS AMONG THREE RANKINGS
OF MEMBER-THERAPIST ACTIVITY DERIVED BY THREE METHODS
OF MEASUREMENT
($N = 17$)

	Ti	Ti/Tg	Ti/(Ti + Ci + Gi)
Ti	—	.88	.85
Ti/Tg		—	.77
Ti/(Ti + Ci + Gi)			—

Since a ranking of members for initial personal adjustment had already been achieved (see Chapter III), it remained to derive measures of hostility and anxiety for the group members in the therapy experience. A method for obtaining hostility and anxiety scores by content analysis of the Rorschach had recently been described and validated by Elizur [21]. On directing that judges score Rorschach protocols by noting the capital letter "A" or "H" when anxiety or hostility was obvious and explicit in responses, while reserving small letter "a" and "h" for responses revealing anxiety or hostility to a lesser degree, Elizur found that graduate student psychologists with no Rorschach training achieved remarkably high agreement, viz., an average correlation coefficient of .77 for eight scorers in noting anxiety scores and of .82 for eight scorers in noting hostility scores. When these scores were related to three independent measures of anxiety and hostility, the author could conclude that the method "appears to be a valid technique for assessment of the subjects' anxiety and hostility. It is a fairly reliable instrument. . . ."

The present study employed the Elizur technique, utilizing the Rorschachs that had been administered prior to the first group meeting. Since Elizur suggested that only Rorschachs containing at least twenty responses be scored in this manner, only the protocols of ten group members were available for use. When these ten were scored by two judges provided with the directions given by Elizur, correlation coefficients of .81 and .76 were yielded for rankings of anxiety and hostility respectively. These relationships are consistent with the findings of Elizur and suggest the reliability of scoring Rorschach protocols for anxiety and hostility in the present study.

Before testing the relationship between quantity of member-therapist role-playing and any of the variables of initial adjustment, anxiety, and hostility, the investigator tested the relationships among the variables. It was important to see if the variables were significantly correlated among themselves. Rankings were prepared for the ten members in the three factors, and Table 22 reports the rank order correlation coefficients which were yielded when the members were ranked for each of the variables. In con-

TABLE 22. RANK ORDER CORRELATION COEFFICIENTS FOR RANKINGS OF 10 GROUP MEMBERS IN THE VARIABLES OF ADJUSTMENT, ANXIETY, AND HOSTILITY

	Anxiety	Hostility	Initial Adjustment
Anxiety	—	.47	−.61
Hostility		—	−.01
Initial Adjustment			—

TABLE 23. RANKINGS OF GROUP MEMBERS IN QUANTITY OF THERAPIST ACTIVITY, INITIAL PERSONAL ADJUSTMENT, HOSTILITY, AND ANXIETY

Code No.	Quantity Member-Therapist Activity Ti/Tg*	Adjustment*	Anxiety*	Hostility*
1	10.5	17	5	8
2	1	3	—	—
3	6.5	2	10	9.5
4	17	12	—	—
5	8	15	3	5
6	10.5	14	—	—
7	2	1	9	4
8	15	10	—	—
9	5	4	7	3
10	9	8	8	9.5
11	12	13	—	—
12	6.5	11	2	1
13	16	9	—	—
14	3	7	4	2
15	14	5	6	7
16	4	16	—	—
17	13	6	1	6

* Rank "1" denotes greatest participation as member-therapist, best personal adjustment, least anxiety, and least hostility, etc.

sideration of ten cases, none of the coefficients is significantly different from zero, for coefficients as large as these could have arisen by chance.[1]

In summary, the preceding section has indicated how rankings of group members were achieved in all the variables to test the hypothesis that there is no significant relationship between the quantity of member-therapist activity and initial personal adjustment, anxiety, and hostility. A validated technique for ranking individuals with respect to anxiety and hostility was used; validation of the initial personal adjustment of group members was described; and a measure of quantity of "T" was sought in three different procedures, each possessing high agreement with the other.

The hypothesis could now be tested. Group member rankings were achieved in *quantity of participation as member-therapist, initial personal adjustment, anxiety, and hostility.* Table 23 summarizes the significant data. As was indicated above, anxiety and hostility rankings were available for only ten group members.

Since three rankings of *quantity* of participation as member-therapist were available, correlation coefficients were computed to test the relationship between initial personal adjustment and each of the participation rankings. When the sums of each member's therapist behavior were ranked (Ti) and this was compared with the ranking of personal adjustment, a rank order correlation coefficient of .26 was obtained. In using the percentage score, Ti/Tg as a basis for ranks, the coefficient was .34. When a ranking of member-therapist participation was derived from the percentage scores, $Ti/(Ti + Ci + Gi)$, the correlation coefficient was .33.[2] None of these correlation coefficients is significantly different from zero, and they could easily have arisen through the accidents of sampling. Moreover, they are not significantly different from one another. Since three methods of deriving quantity of therapist participation scores for ranking yielded values consistently unrelated to initial personal adjustment, the hypothesis that there is no

---

[1] In such small samples, a correlation must be very high to be termed significant. One should guard against erroneously inferring in these events that when a significant correlation is not revealed, the population correlation is zero.

[2] While the therapist activity of the member who had withdrawn from psychotherapy is included in the calculation of these correlation coefficients, the removal of his contribution does not materially alter the results.

relationship between sheer quantity of member-therapist behavior and adjustment is not refuted. The rejection of this null hypothesis is apparently not subject to the method of measurement, since consistent results were obtained in the three procedures outlined above.

It remained to test the relationship between the quantity of member-therapist behavior and the personality variables of anxiety and hostility. When member ranking in anxiety was compared with a single ranking of quantity of therapist participation (Ti/Tg was used for this purpose), the rank order correlation coefficient of —.33 was observed. When member hostility scores were ranked and compared with the same ranking of therapist activity, a coefficient of .57 was yielded. These values are not significantly different from zero and they could have arisen by chance. The hypothesis that no relationship obtains between the quantity of member-therapist activity and the variables (anxiety and hostility) is held to be tenable.

The next procedure was to test the second part of the formulated hypothesis: the *quality* of member-therapist activity is associated with initial personal adjustment, anxiety, and hostility.

Analysis of relationship between quality of member-therapist behavior and the personality variables

It was hypothesized that there would be variable member-therapist behavior beyond what may be explained by recourse to a principle of emulation of the professional therapist. In the sense that the individuals possessing greater personal freedom would behave differently from individuals with less personal freedom, the investigator formulated the question of the association between the quality of member-therapist behavior and the personality variables of initial personal adjustment, anxiety, and hostility. The variables bear upon personal freedom, which enables individuals to entertain a wider variety of behavior toward others and lends them a desire to get closer to others rather than criticize them.

The therapeutic behavior patterns of members should be amenable to differentiation when classification in the three variables is involved. Should group members be separated into classes opposing the initially well-adjusted against the initially poorer-adjusted, the most-anxious against the least-anxious, the most-hostile against the least-hostile, then, predictably, there would be revealed significant differences in patterns of member-therapist behavior between the classes.

Differences in patterns of member-therapist behavior with respect to a classification of initially best-adjusted against initially most-maladjusted were sought first. The procedure involved selecting the five individuals who were best-adjusted and comparing their member-therapist productions with those of the five individuals who were least well-adjusted. The member-therapist behavior pattern chosen for study was the use of "Clarification of Feeling" (T1) through "Reassurance" (T9) against the use of "Evaluation" (T15) through "Disapproval, Criticism" (T16). Categories T1 through T9 were considered as reflecting the desire to get closer to others, while categories T15 through T16 were thought to betray the desire to be critical of others. Specifically, it was hypothesized that significant differences would be observed in the use of the categories upon the classification of members with respect to initial personal adjustment. The null hypothesis is that the mean difference (T15 through T16 minus T1 through T9) for the initially best-adjusted and least-adjusted members is zero.

In the present sample, the five initially best-adjusted group members had a mean difference between T15 through T16 and T1 through T9 of 23.8 with a standard deviation of 6.14, while the five initially least-adjusted group members had a mean difference of 25.6 with a standard deviation of 5.73. Since these standard deviations are not significantly different, the results may be combined to yield $t = .49$. Therefore, it may be concluded that the hypothesis of association between the quality of member-therapist behavior for the entire course of group psychotherapy and initial personal adjustment is rejected. The stated null hypothesis is not refuted.

The question was then posed that significant differences in member-therapist behavior patterns for the best-adjusted and least-adjusted members may be revealed early in psychotherapy. Differences were sought in the use of categories T1 through T9 and T15 through T16 for the first quarter of the experience. Here, the five initially best-adjusted group members had a mean difference between T15 through T16 and T1 through T9 of 11.6 with a standard deviation of 1.51, while the five initially least-adjusted members had a mean difference of 6.0 with a standard deviation of 1.41. Since these standard deviations are not significantly different, the results may be combined to yield $t = 6.02$. When the value is referred to Student's distribution for 8 degrees of freedom, the conclusion is that so large a value of t would occur through the accidents of sampling in less than 1 per 100 samples. The stated null hypothesis is held to be untenable. There is an apparent association between initial personal adjustment and the quality of member-therapist behavior in the early part of psychotherapy. The initially best-adjusted members are characterized by therapist behavior reflecting relatively more positive activity (T1 through T9) and less negative activity (T15 through T16) than the initially least-adjusted members.

On the basis of these data, the investigator offers the tentative formulation that early differences with respect to the quality of member-therapist behavior tend to dissolve as therapy progresses and group members advance toward greater personal adjustment. While the quality of member-therapist behavior early in psychotherapy is differentiated by the quality of initial personal adjustment, the difference disappears as therapy progresses.

It then remained to test the association between anxiety and hostility, and the quality of member-therapist behavior. Again, the behavior pattern chosen for study was the use of "Clarification of Feeling" (T1) through "Reassurance" (T9) against the use of "Evaluation" (T15) through "Disapproval, Criticism" (T16). The procedure involved determining the frequencies in the two categories (T1 through T9 and T15 through T16) for the five most-anxious and the five least-anxious members, and for the five most-hostile and five least-hostile members.

Since the Elizur technique for deriving anxiety and hostility scores from Rorschach content analysis had provided the investigator with rankings of the ten group members in these variables, a decision was made to cut the ranks in half, opposing the top five against the bottom five. In this manner, on inspection of the ranking in anxiety, ranks 1 through 5 were considered as representing the "least-anxious" group of members while ranks 6 through 10 were considered as representing the "most-anxious" group. The same procedure was followed with the rankings of hostility. Consequently, two groups of members were available for both variables (anxiety and hostility) and the pattern of member-therapist behavior (T1 through T9 and T15 through T16) could be studied within these groups. In each case, the null hypothesis is, again, that the mean difference (T15 through T16 minus T1 through T9) for the most-anxious (or most-hostile) and least anxious (or least-hostile) group members is zero.

In the sample, the five least-anxious group members had a mean difference between T15 through T16 and T1 through T9 of 36.6 with a standard deviation of 4.77, while the five most-anxious members had a mean difference of 21.4 with a standard deviation of 7.23. Since these standard deviations are not significantly different, the results may be combined to yield $t = 3.87$. In examining Student's distribution for 8 degrees of freedom, the conclusion is that so large a value of t would occur through the accidents of sampling in less than 1 per 100 samples.

With respect to hostility, the five least-hostile group members had a mean difference between T15 through T16 and T1 through T9 of 37.0 with a standard deviation of 4.12, while the five most-hostile members had a mean difference of 21.0 with a standard deviation of 6.52. Since the standard deviations are not significantly different, the results may be combined to yield $t = 4.64$. For 8 degrees of freedom the conclusion is again that so large a value of t would occur through the accidents of sampling in less than 1 per 100 samples.

It may therefore be held that the null hypothesis (given above) with reference to both variables (anxiety and hostility) is refuted. The less anxious, less hostile members are characterized by therapist behavior reflecting relatively more positive activity (T1 through T9) and less negative activity (T15 through T16) than the most anxious, most hostile members. The quality of therapeutic behavior is significantly differentiated by the personality variables.

Is Therapeutic Gain a Variable Associated with the Quality of Member-Therapist Behavior?

Since gain occurred in the course of the group psychotherapy experiences, an opportunity was provided for testing several hypotheses relative to the phenomenon of gain and its association with the quality of member-therapist behavior. The hypotheses were formulated thus: (1) There is a significant difference in the patterns of member-therapist behavior between a group that profits from psychotherapy and a group that does not profit from the experience. (2) There is a significant difference in the patterns of member-therapist behavior between the halves of group psychotherapy for the profited group of members.

The hypotheses derive from the view that the individual who gains in psychotherapy is lent the capacity to entertain a wider variety of therapeutic responses and a desire to get closer to people rather than to be critical of them. Predictably, a profited group of members' therapeutic behavior should be characterized by relatively more acceptance and permissiveness than disapproval and criticism, and the behavior of a non-profited group should be revealed as possessing the attribute in a significantly different way.

Before proceeding to test the hypotheses, it was necessary to differentiate the classification of gain or profit from psychotherapy from the classification of initial personal adjustment. In order to use gain as a criterion for classifying group members, gain had to be demonstrated as different from personal adjustment.

Chapter III reports how judgments of "profit" or "no-profit" from the therapy experience were validated by comparison with the Incomplete-Sentences Test and the Self-Rating Checklist. The sixteen group members (judgments and test analysis for one member not carried out since he withdrew from therapy rather early) were divided into two groups by this method, one group representing the eight members who profited from therapy, the other representing the eight members who profited little or not at all. The validated ranking of members for initial personal adjustment was arbitrarily cut to form two groups of eight members, one defined as the better-adjusted group, the other considered as the poorer-adjusted group. Table 24 illustrates how the association

TABLE 24. CLASSIFICATION OF 16 MEMBERS IN THE CRITERIA OF INITIAL PERSONAL ADJUSTMENT AND PROFIT FROM PSYCHOTHERAPY

	Most-Profited	Least-Profited
Better-Adjusted	4	4
Poorer-Adjusted	4	4

between gain from therapy and initial personal adjustment could be studied. Although the number of cases is small, challenging the use of the chi-square technique, inspection of the table is useful to the point. As many members who were initially better-adjusted profited as did not; the same is true of those poorer-adjusted. Gain from therapy is differentiated from initial adjustment.

Is There a Difference in the Patterns of Member-Therapist Behavior Between a Group That Profits from Psychotherapy and a Group That Does Not?

To test the hypothesis, the range of member-therapist categories (T1 through T16) was cut at several points. "Clarification of Feeling" (T1) through "Reassurance" (T9) were considered as reflecting behavior of a positive variety; "Opinions" (T10) through "Deflection" (T14) were considered the neutral categories; and "Evaluation" (T15) through "Disapproval, Criticism" (T16) were defined as indicating behavior of a distinctly negative variety.

The frequencies of member-therapist behavior in the two significant classifications (T1 through T9 and T15 through T16) were determined for each individual in both the profited and the non-profited group of members. The null hypothesis was formulated that the mean difference (T15 through T16 minus T1 through T9) for the profited and the non-profited members is zero.

In the sample, the eight individuals who profited from psychotherapy had a mean difference between T15 through T16 and T1 through T9 of 40.5 with a standard deviation of 5.92, while the eight individuals who did not profit had a mean difference of 29.5 with a standard deviation of 8.28. Since the standard deviations are not significantly different, the results may be combined to yield $t = 3.03$. A t value of this size occurs through the accidents of sampling in less than 1 per 100 samples from the hypothetical population, and the null hypothesis is rejected. The investigator concludes that different patterns of therapist behavior obtain among members who profit from group psychotherapy and among members who do not profit from the experience. The behavior of the former group, in contrast to the latter, is characterized by the use of relatively more positive member-therapist activity (T1 through T9) and less negative (T15 through T16).

To press the issue further, the hypothesis was formulated that nondirective member-therapist behavior (T1 through T3) would increase significantly in the profited group and it would not rise in the non-profited group. Figure 4 graphs the use of the classifica-

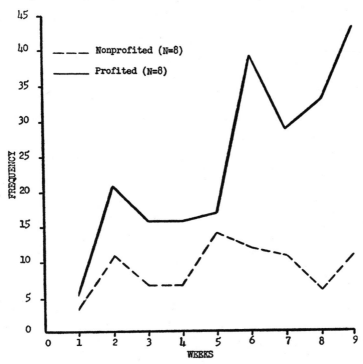

FIGURE 4. FREQUENCY IN USE OF NONDIRECTIVE BEHAVIOR, CATEGORIES T1–T3, BY MEMBER-THERAPISTS OVER THE WEEKS OF PSYCHOTHERAPY IN THE PROFITED AND NON-PROFITED GROUPS OF MEMBERS

tion, T1 through T3, by the profited and non-profited groups over the weeks of psychotherapy. While this method of data analysis may be cruder than other statistical techniques, the difference in member-therapist behavior as reflected in the graph is striking. Although the profited-group's use of the classification rises steadily through the course of psychotherapy, a best-fitting straight line to the behavior of the non-profited group would not be significantly different from a line whose slope is zero. On the basis of these data, significant differences in the patterns of member-therapist behavior for groups of profited and non-profited members are demonstrated.

*Is There a Difference in the Patterns of Member-
Therapist Behavior Between the Halves of Psychotherapy for the Profited Group of Members?*

If the changes in perception of the members in the profited
group occur, it was considered possible to demonstrate changes in
behavior (member-therapist behavior) in the course of therapy. It
was hypothesized that a profited group would behave differently in
the two halves of psychotherapy while a non-profited group would
not show this significant change in member-therapist activity. Predictably the profited group should be characterized by change
indicating more sensitiveness to others and less criticism of others
(frequencies of therapist behavior should increase at the high end
of the scale of "T" and decrease at the low end of "T").

The hypothesis was tested in the classifications T1 through T9,
and T15 through T16. Again the possible range of member-therapist behavior was cut at several points to define two significant
broad classifications of positive (T1 through T9) and negative
(T15 through T16) therapeutic reaction.

When the hypothesis tested is that the population mean difference (in the non-profited group of eight members' use of T1
through T9 in the first and second halves of psychotherapy) is zero,
a value of $t = .67$ is observed for the sample mean difference of 2.7.
It may be concluded that the hypothesis is not rejected, for a t
value of this magnitude could easily have arisen by chance. On
testing the hypothesis that the population mean difference is zero
for the non-profited members' use of T15 through T16 in the first
and second halves of psychotherapy, a value of $t = 1.67$ is yielded
for the sample mean difference of 1.6. Here, as before, the conclusion is that a t value of this magnitude could easily have arisen
through the accidents of sampling. One cannot conclude that the
pattern of member-therapist behavior for the non-profited group
changes significantly in the course of psychotherapy. The hypothesis that the behavior of a non-profited group does not change is
consistent with the theoretical view and is not refuted on examination of the quantitative data.

On the other hand, consideration of the same problem within
a profited group yields significant differences in the pattern of

member-therapist behavior between the halves of psychotherapy. When the null hypothesis is tested for the classification T1 through T9, a value of $t = 3.72$ is observed for a sample mean difference of 15.1. When this is referred to Student's distribution for 7 degrees of freedom, the conclusion is that so large a value would occur through the accidents of sampling in less than 1 per 100 samples. On testing the hypothesis for the classification T15 through T16, a value of $t = 7.16$ is yielded for a sample mean difference of 9.1. Here again the conclusion is that the mean difference is highly significant. The behavior pattern for the profited group is revealed as evolving toward an increase in positive activity (T1 through T9) and a decrease in negative activity (T15 through T16). This is consistent with the theoretical view and it finds support in quantified data.

PREDICTABILITY OF THE QUANTITY AND QUALITY OF MEMBER-THERAPIST BEHAVIOR

Since significant differences were obtained in the quality of member-therapist behavior with respect to the personality variables of initial personal adjustment, anxiety, and hostility, the Rorschach which was used as a method for deriving scores in the personality attributes can be employed in a limited way to predict the quality of behavior in a group psychotherapy experience. Predictably, the behavior of the initially better-adjusted or less-anxious or less-hostile individual will be characterized by a relatively greater capacity to entertain a wider variety of activity and a desire to be more sensitive to and accepting of others. In this way, a measure of initial personal adjustment derived from Rorschach psychograms and measures of anxiety and hostility from Rorschach content analysis (the Elizur technique) predict the quality of therapeutic behavior for group members.

Although no relationship was discovered between the quantity of therapeutic behavior and the personality variables, it was felt that quantity of member-therapist participation would be useful to predict. This might very well be used as a criterion for composing groups in psychotherapy. Although the literature is replete with criteria for organizing groups (see Chapter II), the concept of quantity of participation has escaped examination. Since the extent of participation may have important consequences in the group, the investigator considered that it would be worth while to foretell by some index or measure.

It was hypothesized that the quantity of member-therapist activity would be related to some measure of the general activity level of the individual. In Rorschach R (number of responses on the Rorschach Test), it was assumed that such a measure was available. R can be viewed as an expression of the general activity level of an individual that would signify his behavioral activity in other situations. It is, in fact, used as a measure of productivity in standard Rorschach interpretation.

To test the hypothesis, Rorschach R's for the sixteen group members who were tested were ranked. This ranking was then correlated with the three rankings of member-therapist participation as defined above (p. 69). When the rank order correlation coefficients were calculated, consistent relationships were observed between R and each of the three methods of deriving ranks in quantity of member-therapist behavior. The coefficient between the ranking of quantity based on Ti and R was .73; the relationship between the ranking derived from the scores Ti/Tg and R was .78; and the coefficient based upon Ti/(Ti + Ci + Gi) and R was .53. The values of the three correlation coefficients are not significantly different from each other but they are all significantly different from zero. The investigator concludes that the test measure, R, is useful in predicting the quantity of member-therapist behavior. Table 25 summarizes the relationships.

TABLE 25. Rank Order Correlation Coefficients Between Three Rankings of Quantity of Member-Therapist Behavior and Rorschach R (Number of Responses)
($N = 16$)

Rho R, Ti	.73
Rho R, Ti/Tg	.72
Rho R, Ti/(Ti + Ci + Gi)	.53

The question arose with regard to the possibility that Rorschach R was related as well to a group member's total activity in the therapy experience. Total activity is defined as an individual's participation as "Client" (C), "Therapist" (T), and "General Intellectualizer" (G). To test this hypothesis, the total participation of group members was ranked by two methods. It was important to show that the obtained relationship was not related to the method of measurement but that consistent results could be derived in several ways. One ranking of group members' total participation was yielded by utilizing the scores $(Ci + Ti + Gi)$. That is, each member's contribution as client, therapist, and general contributor was summated. Another ranking was derived by computing the percentage $(Ci + Ti + Gi)/(Cg + Tg + Gg)$ for each group member which represented his share of the total participation in his group.

When rankings based on the two methods of describing total participation were established and correlated with the ranking of Rorschach R, significant relationships were observed. The rank order correlation coefficient between R and $(Ci + Ti + Gi)$ was .63, while the coefficient between R and $(Ci + Ti + Gi)/(Cg + Tg + Gg)$ was .68. These values are not significantly different from each other but they are significantly different from zero. The hypothesis that Rorschach R is related to total member participation in group therapy experiences is held tenable. While R is useful in predicting the quantity of member-therapist behavior, it is also useful in predicting total group participation as well.

CERTAIN DYNAMICS CHARACTERIZING THE PHENOMENON OF MEMBER-THERAPIST BEHAVIOR

Several other hypotheses relating to the dynamic interplay of member behavior were investigated. They were especially concerned with interactive behavior.

Is the Quality of a Specific Member-Therapist's Behavior Toward Another Group Member Associated with His Personal Feelings Toward That Member?

The hypothesis was advanced that the quality of a member's therapeutic behavior toward another in his group would be associated with his own personal feelings toward the member. Considering the entire range of possible member-therapist activity (T1 through T16), it was felt that an individual would utilize a different pattern of activity toward the person he liked than toward the person he disliked. Therapist behavior directed toward the "liked" person should be characterized by relatively more acceptance and permissiveness and less clash opinion, disapproval, and criticism, while the alternate pattern should be revealed as directed toward the "disliked" person.

It was for this reason that members' judgments concerning other members had been sought. In the original design of the research, a sociometric technique had been devised to afford the investigator information about the feelings of group members for one another. The plan was conceived to have these forms executed at regular intervals in post-meeting sessions of five minutes' duration. Although it was withdrawn early in the research because members expressed considerable resistance to its use, it was in fact administered several times.

These data, available in Group B, offered an opportunity to test the hypothesis. In her executions of the sociometric technique, member number 7 had consistently reported herself as liking member number 8 most and member number 9 least. Since member 7 was an active member-therapist, her behavior in themes in which those she liked and disliked were clients (behaving as "C") could be studied. Consequently, member 7's therapist behavior was calculated for the first four themes in which member 8 behaved as client and for the first four themes in which member 9 behaved as client.

Table 26 reports the frequencies of member number 7's therapist behavior in two broad classifications (T1 through T10 and T10W through T16) as the behavior was directed against member number 8 (an individual in the group whom she liked) and member number 9 (an individual she disliked). The pattern of member-therapist activity chosen for study involved the broad classifications from "Clarification of Feeling" (T1) through "Opin-

TABLE 26. FREQUENCIES IN TWO CLASSIFICATIONS OF MEMBER-THERAPIST BEHAVIOR FOR MEMBER NO. 7, DIRECTED TOWARD A "LIKED" GROUP MEMBER AND A "DISLIKED" GROUP MEMBER

	T1–T10	T10W–T16
Toward Member "Liked"	31	16
Toward Member "Disliked"	15	47

Chi-square   19.12

ion" (T10) and from "Clash Opinion" (T10W) through "Disapproval, Criticism" (T16). Although the cut-off point is necessarily arbitrary, it has a rationale in that T1 through T10 might be assumed to be therapist behavior of an accepting kind, while T10W through T16 might be viewed as non-accepting and rejecting. When the hypothesis tested is that the populations ("liked" and "disliked" group members) have the same proportion in the various classes (T1 through T10 and T10W through T16) a chi-square of 19.12 is observed. This value is significant at the .01 level, and the hypothesis is rejected. The alternate hypothesis that the personal feelings of a member differentiate the pattern of his therapist activity is held to be confirmed.

To lend further support to the finding, the therapist behavior of member number 7 was calculated as directed against two other members whom she reported herself as liking. Should the therapist

TABLE 27. FREQUENCIES IN TWO CLASSIFICATIONS OF MEMBER-THERAPIST BEHAVIOR FOR MEMBER NO. 7, DIRECTED TOWARD TWO "LIKED" GROUP MEMBERS

	T1–T10	T10W–T16
Toward Member "Liked" (No. 8)	31	16
Toward Member "Liked" (No. 11)	48	34

Chi-square 0.69

patterns directed against two "liked" members not be differentiated, this fact would lend weight to the original hypothesis. Table 27 reports the frequencies of member number 7's behavior as directed against members 8 and 11. A chi-square of 0.69 yielded by these values is not significant; differences of this order could arise by chance. This is interpreted as lending support to the association between the member-therapist pattern that an individual directs toward another member and his personal feelings toward the member.

Does the Quality of Member-Therapist Behavior Differentiate the Quality of Client Behavior?

The hypothesis was formulated that threatening member-therapist behavior induces a different pattern of client response than therapist behavior of a less threatening (accepting) variety. The theory in personality and therapy in which the present research is oriented views the individual as, in part, a defending organism. Threat, in the form of "interpretation," "evaluation," "disapproval," and "clash opinion," is said to induce personality defense, while acceptance in the form of "clarification of feeling," "restatement of content," "empathy," and "approval" is considered as disarming and encouraging to the individual to explore himself and his world.

Data were available to offer some quantitative evidence for the hypothesis that threatening member-therapist behavior induces different patterns of client response than does less threatening therapist behavior. Therapist categories had been ranked on a continuum from the least to the most threatening verbal behavior. Client categories had been ranked from the most to the least therapeutically positive in the sense that those client categories at the higher end of the scale indicated a greater tendency to elaboration and exploration, while those at the lower end of the scale indicated constricting, defensive behavior.

The hypothesis was attacked by examining the transcribed and coded protocols of the group sessions and determining the category of client response following upon member-therapist behavior, "Clarification of Feeling" (T1) through "Opinion" (T10) and "Clash Opinion" (T10W) through "Disapproval, Criticism" (T16). The therapist categories were to be considered as broad divisions of "threat" and "no-threat." Another decision was made to consider "Discussion of Plans" (C1) through "Acceptance of Interpretation" (C11) and "Ambivalent Acceptance of Interpretation" (C12) through "Negative Attitude Toward Self" (C22) as broad categories reflecting more versus less self-exploration and elaboration of problem.

Table 28 reports the tabulated client category sequels (C1 through C11 and C12 through C22) to the therapist categories (T1 through T10 and T10W through T16) in the three psychotherapy groups. In testing the hypothesis it was not considered necessary to utilize the entire population of protocols, so a sample of sessions was analyzed for each psychotherapy group. Systematically, the first, fourth, seventh, tenth, thirteenth, etc., sessions were tabulated.

TABLE 28. CLIENT BEHAVIOR ("C") IN TWO CLASSIFICATIONS FOLLOWING UPON MEMBER-THERAPIST BEHAVIOR ("T") IN TWO CLASSIFICATIONS IN THE THREE PSYCHOTHERAPY GROUPS

| | GROUP A | | GROUP B | | GROUP C | |
	T1–T10	T10W–T16	T1–T10	T10W–T16	T1–T10	T10W–T16
C1–C11	90	59	73	26	48	41
C12–C22	37	185	16	97	26	78
Chi-squares	75.75		83.66		17.06	

When the hypothesis tested is that various classifications (T1 through T10 and T10W through T16) have the same proportion in the various classes (C1 through C11 and C12 through C22) chi-squares of 75.75, 83.66, and 17.06 are observed for Groups A, B, and C respectively. In rejecting the hypothesis, the alternate is held to be tenable in that significantly different patterns of client behavior follow upon different categories of member-therapist behavior. Interpretively, less threatening therapist behavior induces more exploratory client behavior than does more threatening therapist behavior.

CHAPTER VI

AN ANALYSIS OF THE ROLE OF THE LEADER

Earl F. Telschow

This section of the research project concerned itself with an examination of the behavior of the group leader as he interacted with the group members. Hypotheses were tested regarding the nature of the leader's participation and how it contributed to the general process of therapy as well as to certain outcomes experienced by the members. In this connection, it was thought profitable to tabulate the leader's responses so as to preserve their quality and direction in terms of the members with whom he interacted. Member responses subsequent to leader responses were tabulated in a similar manner. In this way group leader responses toward each member as well as member responses following specific leader responses were available for examination.

The hypotheses which suggested themselves fell into two broad categories: the *quantity* of group leader responses seem related to certain variables, and the *quality* of group leader responses tend to differentiate the quality of group member responses. In approaching the problem from this point of view, various sub-hypotheses were formulated and as many variables were examined as was feasible. Consequently, such factors as the initial adjustment of the members, degree of gain from the experience, and specific constellations of group member behavior were studied in relation to the two major hypotheses.

It was hoped that this section of the research might offer some tentative answers, or at least clues, to the role of the leader in this form of psychotherapy. Is there an optimum amount of leader participation? Do certain kinds of leader statements tend to be associated with client verbal release? Does the leader tend to interact differently with those who gain most from therapy? These are some of the basic questions that seemed to merit investigation.

OVERVIEW OF LEADER BEHAVIOR

Before discussing the specific hypotheses tested in this study, an over-all view of the quantity, quality, and extent of group leader participation in each of the three groups is presented.

Table 29 shows the relative proportion of group leader categories used by each of the three group leaders throughout the group therapy series. It will be noted from the table that in all three groups over 75 percent of all group leader responses fell into three categories: simple acceptance, restatement of content,

TABLE 29. RELATIVE PROPORTION, IN TERMS OF PERCENTAGE, OF GROUP LEADER CATEGORIES USED BY EACH OF THE THREE GROUP LEADERS THROUGHOUT EACH GROUP THERAPY SERIES

Leader Category	Leader A	Leader B	Leader C
1. Simple Acceptance	.369	.226	.226
2. Restatement of Content	.284	.470	.381
3. Clarification of Feeling (general)	.133	.168	.164
Totals for 1, 2, 3	.786	.864	.771
4. Clarifying Negative Feeling Toward Self	.054	.034	.037
5. Clarifying Positive Feeling Toward Self	.028	.024	.009
6. Clarifying Ambivalent Feeling Toward Self	.001	.003	.004
7. Clarifying Negative Feeling Toward Others	.022	.011	.011
8. Clarifying Positive Feeling Toward Others	.003	.006	.002
9. Clarifying Ambivalent Feeling Toward Others	.000	.000	.000
10. Clarifying a Group Feeling	.009	.007	.011
11. Clarifying Divergent Feelings Between Members	.002	.001	.004
Totals for 4 through 11	.119	.086	.078
12. Nondirective Lead	.005	.010	.029
13. Clarifying Question	.012	.005	.004
14. Structuring	.040	.004	.033
15. Giving Information	.012	.011	.017
16. Summarizing Statement	.003	.000	.044
17. Forcing a Member to Develop a Topic	.003	.000	.000
18. Direct Question	.002	.001	.000
19. Friendly Discussion	.012	.010	.020
20. Unclassifiable	.006	.002	.000
21. Humor	.000	.007	.004
Grand Totals	1.000	1.000	1.000

and clarification of feeling. The latter category, as has been mentioned, was subdivided into finer definitions. However, a brief examination of the table reveals that categories 4 through 11 were utilized very rarely by the group leaders. In fact the tabulated frequencies for these categories were so small that statistical procedures could seldom be used. This circumstance may be partially accounted for by the fact that it often proved impossible to judge the quality and direction of feelings expressed by the members. Consequently, the more general category of clarification of feeling (CF) had to be assigned in practically all instances. Since it proved almost impossible to differentiate expressed feelings according to these finer subdivisions, the frequencies were combined with the more general category (CF) for most purposes of calculation.

Further examination of Table 29 reveals that the proportion of group leader categories utilized varied considerably from group to group. This variability may be explained partially by the differing personalities in each of the groups. That is, to a large extent the quality of group leader participation is determined by the quality of member participation. For example, if members do not feel free to express attitudes and feelings, the group leader must confine his responses to a paraphrasing of the essential content of member discourse. The variability in use of simple acceptance may be explained, however, since group leaders B and C expressed acceptance of client verbalizations by nodding to a greater extent than did group leader A. Such nonverbal behavior could not, of course, be recorded, and consequently the figures in Table 29 for simple acceptance are not truly indicative of the use of that category of leader behavior.

Although group leader categories were employed with considerable variability, nondirective responses were used almost exclusively. Those categories which might be considered directive (direct questions, giving information, and forcing client to develop a topic) had a mean use of less than 2 percent of all group leader responses. Thus, 98 percent of all responses used by the three group leaders seem clearly nondirective.

One of the factors limiting the conclusions which may be drawn from this study is the decidedly restricted range of therapist behavior. Thus, results are likely to be less clear-cut than if two quite different methods of therapy were compared. It should be kept in mind, therefore, that the positive results were obtained in a situation where therapist differences were actually very small.

Part of the therapeutic benefit from group therapy is thought to result from the social interaction of the members. In the beginning sessions it is to be expected that the group leader may have to participate to a considerable extent since the members are not well enough acquainted to interact freely. However, as the sessions progress one might expect, at least in this type of therapy, that the members might interact increasingly and that leader participation would consequently diminish.

Graphs were made showing the extent of group leader participation over time for each of the three groups. Plots were based on the proportion of group leader responses to the total responses of each session.

Although there seemed to be a rather clear tendency for the quantity of group leader A's participation to decrease as the sessions progressed, no such tendency was observed for the other two group leaders. The possibility suggested itself, however, that particular kinds of group leader response may assume a sort of pattern over time even though the gross amount of leader participation does not seem to vary in any consistent manner with time. Similar graphs were constructed to illustrate any observable trends over time in the proportion of group leader responses in the three main categories: simple acceptance, restatement of content, and clarification of feeling.

These graphs showed no definable pattern over time in the use of these specific categories by the three group leaders. One is forced to the conclusion that the use of group leader categories in this study varies considerably from group to group and that no clear-cut patterns emerge.

THE QUANTITY OF GROUP LEADER PARTICIPATION

It was hypothesized that the gross amount of interaction between the group leader and the members is related to certain variables within the total structure of the groups. The testing of subhypotheses under this general heading involved an examination of group leader responses directed toward particular members.

The Initial Adjustment of the Members

One hypothesis that suggests itself is that there is no relationship between the initial health or adjustment of the members and the amount of group leader interaction. To test this hypothesis, the seventeen members were ranked in terms of their initial adjustment according to the method described in Chapter III. Then, the total amount of group leader interaction with each member was calculated. A ranking of the members according to the amount that each was interacted with the group leader was then made. This ranking was based on the percentage of total group leader responses directed toward specific members. A positive rank order correlation of .103 was calculated from these figures. Since this correlation value is not significantly different from zero, no relationship has been found to exist between the initial health or adjustment of a member and the extent of the group leader's interaction with that member in this study. The findings, therefore, do not permit the rejection of the hypothesis that there is no relation between the initial health or adjustment of the members and the extent of leader participation.

The Relative Activity of the Members

A second hypothesis that the quantity of group leader participation may be related to certain variables may be stated in this fashion: there is no relationship between the amount that a group leader interacts with a given member and that member's position in terms of the amount that he is active in the group. That is, those members who participate most in the groups may or may not be those to whom the group leader responds most. In an effort to test the null hypothesis, a ranking of the seventeen members was obtained according to the amount that they participated in each group. This was accomplished by computing the proportion of total member responses attributable to each member of each group. Similarly, the proportion of total group leader responses directed toward each of the members of each group was calculated. The resulting percentages provided a method of ranking the members in terms of the extent of group leader interaction with each one. A positive correlation coefficient of .860 between these two rankings was obtained, which differs significantly from zero. Consequently, the hypothesis that there is no relationship between the amount that a group leader interacts with a given member and that member's position in terms of the amount that he is active in the group is rejected.

Discordant Member Behavior

Another variable to be examined involves discordant behavior of the group members. The hypothesis is stated in this fashion: there is no relationship between the extent of group leader participation and the discordant behavior of the members. This hypothesis arose from clinical experience in which it was noticed that when the leader was particularly inactive, the members were apt to become defensive toward each other. Apparently one of the functions of a group leader is to act as a sort of buffer between group member feelings. When left to their own devices, members may become somewhat critical of each other, resorting to defensive remarks, attempts to deflect the subject of discourse away from themselves, expressions of confusion, and other responses indicating that considerable tension or conflict has arisen. Discordant behavior among the members, however, may be looked upon as a measure of the extent to which the leader is willing to follow the group rather than steer the meetings.

To test the hypothesis that no relationship exists between the extent of leader participation and discordant member behavior, each session was ranked in each group according to the percentage of discordant member behavior exhibited. Those member responses believed to indicate discord or confliflct were: defensive remarks (C19), deflection (C20), rejection of interpretation (C15), rejection of opinion (C16), evaluation (T15), clash opinion (T10-W), and intellectual counter-discussion (G6W). These categories were selected by agreement among the investigators. The sessions in each group were again ranked in terms of the relative activity of the group leaders. Figures for this ranking were obtained by calculating, for each session, the proportion of the total responses attributable to the leader. Rank order correlations calculated from the above data resulted in the following coefficients: Group A = .113, Group B = .714, and Group C = .409. Although these values tend in the same direction, the correlation coefficient obtained in Group B is the only one found to be significantly different from zero.

The above findings are interesting when compared with the figures in Table 30. This table shows the extent to which each group leader was active in each group, as well as the percentage of discordant member behavior in each group. The latter figures were obtained by calculating the proportion of total member responses considered discordant.

TABLE 30. PERCENTAGE OF DISCORDANT MEMBER BEHAVIOR AND EXTENT OF LEADER PARTICIPATION IN EACH OF THE GROUPS

	Percentage of Leader Responses	Percentage of Discordant Member Behavior
Group A	.159	.125
Group B	.228	.037
Group C	.178	.104

The figures in Table 30 demonstrate that the group in which the leader was most active, B, contained the smallest proportion of discordant behavior among the members. Group leader A, the least active, had the largest proportion of discordant behavior in his group.

Other factors, such as the differing personalities of the members in each group and the differing personalities of the leaders, probably entered into the apparent relationship, but it is perhaps safe to assume that at least part of the discordant member behavior can be associated with or related to the extent of group leader participation in the groups. Although the evidence is not consistently conclusive, doubt is placed on the hypothesis that there is no relationship between the extent of leader participation and discordant behavior among the members. Future research studies might do well to explore this hypothesis and perhaps make an effort to control more of the variables involved.

Member Gain from Therapy

Another hypothesis examined concerned the quantity of leader participation involving the most- and least-profited groups: there is no difference in the extent to which the group leaders interacted with those who gained most and those who gained least from therapy. One might expect that those who gained most were the ones to whom the leaders directed a larger proportion of their responses. To test the null hypothesis, the percentage of each group leader's responses directed toward each member in his group was computed. The mean percentage of group leader responses for the two "gained" groups was obtained. In this way the two "gained" groups were compared according to the extent of leader participation with the members of each. When the hypothesis is tested that the population mean difference is zero, a value of $t = .151$ is observed for the sample mean difference of .007. When the value is referred to Student's distribution for 15 degrees of freedom, the conclusion is that so large a value of t would occur through the accidents of sampling in more than 5 per 100 samples from the hypothetical population. The null hypothesis is not refuted. Consequently, there is no evidence to suggest that the group leaders directed a greater proportion of remarks to the most-profited group.

Although there seems to be no difference between the two "gained" groups in the extent of leader participation, it seemed profitable to investigate the possibility that differences may exist in the use of specific leader techniques directed toward the two groups. Consequently, the following hypothesis was tested: there is no difference in the frequency of specific leader categories directed toward the two "gained" groups.

Frequencies of the three main leader categories directed toward the members of each "gained" group were tabulated and the resulting data were subjected to t-test analysis.

When the hypothesis is tested that the population mean difference (in the leaders' use of simple acceptance toward the two "gained" groups) is zero, a value of $t = .23$ is observed for the sample mean difference of 3.4. When the value is referred to Student's distribution, the conclusion is that so large a value of t would occur through the accidents of sampling in more than 5 per 100 samples from the hypothetical population. The hypothesis that the mean difference is zero cannot be rejected.

An examination of restatement of content directed toward the two "gained" groups yields a mean difference of 20.1 and a value of $t = 1.04$. Reference to Student's distribution indicates that such a value of t could have occurred through accidents of sampling in more than 5 per 100 samples from the hypothetical population. Consequently, the null hypothesis is not refuted. In terms of actual frequency the group leaders directed considerably more restatement of content responses to the most-profited group. However, the statistical analysis just reviewed places serious doubt on the idea that this is a reliable difference.

A mean difference of .75 is observed between the two "gained" groups when analysis is made of the leaders' use of clarification of feeling. This sample mean difference yields a value of $t = .07$. Consequently, the null hypothesis cannot be rejected.

So far as this study is concerned, there is no evidence to indicate that there are real differences in the frequency of specific leader categories directed toward the two "gained" groups.

To summarize, there is no apparent relationship in this study between the amount of group leader interaction with a particular member and that member's relative position in terms of initial adjustment. However, a significantly positive association has been found to exist between the amount of leader interaction with a specific member and that member's relative position according to the amount he is active within the groups. Although the results are not consistently significant, a trend is noticed for discordant member behavior to vary inversely with the extent of leader participation in a given session. There seems to be no real differences in the extent of gross group leader participation between the most- and least-profited groups. Moreover, leaders do not appear to direct specific kinds of responses to the two groups in a differential manner.

THE QUALITY OF GROUP LEADER PARTICIPATION

This section is organized to investigate another fundamental point: the quality of group leader participation tends to differentiate the quantity and quality of member responses. That is, the quality and quantity of member responses are associated with particular kinds of leader responses. The testing of this major hypothesis required that subhypotheses of a more specific nature be subjected to statistical analysis.

Client Release Units

It is a common clinical observation that clients seem to experience considerable release from the mere fact that they feel free enough to express themselves at length during the therapeutic hour. Indeed, the amount of verbal flow in itself may have beneficial effects. An examination of therapy protocols immediately reveals that some client responses are long and others are relatively short. Are there certain types of group leader response which seem to facilitate, or at least be followed by, verbal flow more readily than others? The specific hypothesis to be tested is stated as follows: there are no significant differences in the proportion of client release units following various group leader categories of behavior. In attempting to test this hypothesis a tabulation was made of the extent of client verbalization immediately following certain group leader techniques. An arbitrary division point had to be established to obtain relative measures of client verbalization. It was decided that five or more lines of uninterrupted client dialogue would be termed a release unit and less than this amount of client verbalization (a nonrelease unit) would be used for comparative purposes. Since it is largely the leader's choice whether or not silences are allowed to develop in group therapy, pauses have been included as a group leader technique.

The four group leader techniques which were examined are: simple acceptance, restatement of content, clarification of feeling, and pause. Using the *t*-test, every possible paired combination was examined to ascertain which techniques differed significantly. That is, simple acceptance was compared with restatement of content, then with clarification of feeling, and then with pause, etc. With but two exceptions, to be described immediately below, no real differences were found.

When clarification of feeling was compared with pause in the proportion of release units which followed them, a percentage mean difference of .10 was calculated. This resulted in a value of $t = 2.73$. Inspection of Student's distribution reveals that this value is significant at the 5 percent level of confidence. For this particular pair of leader techniques, then, serious doubt is placed on the hypothesis that no real difference exists in the proportion of client release units which follow them. Examination of the means reveals that pause was followed by a larger proportion of release units.

A comparison of restatement of content and pause results in a percentage mean difference of .11 and a value of $t = 2.36$. Such a value of t would occur through sampling errors in less than 5 per 100 samples. Consequently, the hypothesis that the mean difference is zero is held to be untenable. Here again, the means indicate that pause was followed by a greater proportion of release units.

These findings differ somewhat, at least at first glance, from what one might expect. Nondirective therapists have long assumed that clarification of feeling was especially productive of client release. The data in this study seem to indicate that there is no apparent difference between restatement of content and clarification of feeling nor between simple acceptance and clarification of feeling. Indeed, pauses seem to be followed by client verbal release more often than do other techniques.

A partial explanation of the above results suggests itself. Freedom of expression seems closely related to the amount of perceived threat in a situation. It is possible that pauses are perceived as less threatening and consequently do not inhibit verbal flow as much as do other leader techniques. However, it is also true that pauses are most likely to be used by the leader when it is rather obvious that the client intends to go on and talk more. Restatement of content and clarification of feeling, on the other hand, are more likely to be employed when a client has finished expressing some idea or feeling. Thus it may be somewhat hazardous to suggest that pauses are less threatening than other techniques.

Therapeutic Gain and Client Release Units

The assumption that verbal release is beneficial suggests a hypothesis related to the findings in the preceding section: there is no significant difference between the most-profited and least-profited groups in the frequency of client release units following group leader techniques. Frequencies of all client release units following group leader techniques were tabulated for the two "gained" groups. These data were subjected to t-test analysis.

The calculated mean difference between the most-profited and least-profited groups in terms of frequency of release units following leader techniques was 24.75. The standard deviations of the two groups were computed and they were not found to differ significantly from each other. Consequently, the results may be combined to yield $t = 1.95$. Although this closely approaches the 5 percent level of confidence, the null hypothesis cannot be refuted. Hence, although an examination of the frequencies shows that the most-profited group reacted to leader techniques with over twice as many release units, it cannot be concluded that this is a real or significant difference.

Leader Techniques and "Good" Client Responses

It was assumed that client responses immediately following group leader techniques might vary in quality according to the quality of precedent leader behavior. The hypothesis may be stated as follows: there are no differences in the frequency of good client responses following various leader categories. The method of ranking the twenty-two client categories in terms of movement toward adjustment has been described in Chapter III. The "good" or upper end of this scale contains client categories that reflect relatively healthy patterns of behavior, e.g., discussion of plans, insight and understanding, positive attitudes toward the self. The lower end of this continuum reflects poorer patterns of behavior from an adjustment standpoint, e.g., defensive behavior, rejection of advice, negative attitudes toward the self. In a sense, then, client categories have been arranged in quality from good to poor. For comparison purposes an arbitrary division point on this scale was selected at C12 (ambivalent acceptance of interpretation). Hence, frequency of client responses following leader techniques was tabulated for the C1 through C11 categories. These frequencies were tabulated in reference to the specific types of group leader behavior which they followed. Thus, paired comparisons were made between all possible combinations of the following group leader techniques: simple acceptance, restatement of content, clarification of feeling, and pause.

A comparison between simple acceptance and restatement of content for the frequency of good client response which followed them for each group member resulted in a mean difference of 34.53 and a value of $t = 2.89$. Since this value of t could have occurred through chance factors in less than 5 per 100 samples, the null hypothesis regarding this particular pair of leader techniques is held to be untenable. Examination of the means reveals that restatement of content was more often followed by good client responses.

When simple acceptance is compared with clarification of feeling, a mean difference of 21.24 is observed resulting in a value of $t = 3.24$, which is found to be significant at the 5 percent level of confidence. The null hypothesis regarding these two leader techniques, then, is held to be untenable. In this case more good client responses follow clarification of feeling.

A mean difference of 6.24 was observed between simple acceptance and pause. This resulted in a value of $t = 1.48$, which, according to Student's distribution, could easily have occurred through accidents of sampling in more than 5 per 100 samples. Hence, in this case, the null hypothesis is not refuted. Apparently simple acceptance and pause were not productive of good client responses in a differential manner.

When restatement of content is compared with clarification of feeling, a mean difference of 15.53 is observed resulting in a value of $t = 2.24$, which could have occurred through accidents of sampling in less than 5 per 100 samples. Thus, the null hypothesis is held to be untenable. Comparison of the means indicates that restatement of content was more often followed by good client responses.

A mean difference of 34.88 was found between restatement of content and pause, resulting in a value of $t = 3.28$, which is significant at the 5 percent level of confidence. Consequently, the hypothesis that no real difference exists between these two leader techniques is rejected. Inspection of the means reveals that restatement of content was more often followed by good client responses.

Finally, a mean difference of 21.88 was computed between clarification of feeling and pause, resulting in a value of $t = 3.36$. Such a value of t could not have occurred through accidents of sampling in more than 5 per 100 samples. Consequently, the hypothesis that the mean difference is zero is rejected. The means indicate that clarification of feeling was followed by a greater number of good client responses.

It seems possible to conclude from the above data that restatement of content and clarification of feeling are consistently followed by greater numbers of good client responses than either simple acceptance or pause. This apparent finding needs considerably more confirmation by future studies before it can be regarded as anything but suggestive and tentative. The idea that the quality of leader response tends to differentiate the quality of member response immediately following cannot be answered definitively in this study.

Quality of Client Response and Therapeutic Gain

If the ranking of client responses in terms of adjustment is valid, one would expect a greater number of client responses in the C1 through C11 categories following leader techniques in the most-profited group. The hypothesis may be stated in this fashion: there is no difference between the number of client responses in the good (C1 through C11) and poor (C12 through C22) categories following group leader techniques for the two "gained" groups. To test this hypothesis, client responses immediately following group leader techniques were again examined in terms of their quality (C1 through C11 and C12 through C22).

Differences were sought in the use of categories C1 through C11 and C12 through C22, following leader techniques for the two "gained" groups. The eight members in the most-profited group had a mean difference between C1 through C11 and C12 through C22 of 144.63, while the eight members in the least-profited group had a mean difference of 80.5. Since the obtained standard deviations were not found to differ significantly, the results may be combined to yield a value of $t = 1.44$. Student's distribution reveals that such a value of t would occur through the accidents of sampling in more than 5 per 100 samples. Consequently, the null hypothesis cannot be rejected. Although the data tend in the expected direction, it must be concluded that there is no real difference between "gained" groups in the number of C1 through C11 and C12 through C22 client categories following leader responses.

Threatened Client Behavior

The concept of threat assumes great importance in the phenomenological and nondirective approaches to understanding psychotherapy, and consequently deserves attention in a research of this nature. Although nondirective therapy attempts to establish a nonthreatening atmosphere, it is highly improbable that it can ever eliminate perceived threat completely. Furthermore, it seems a reasonable assumption that certain types of group leader behavior may be followed by greater amounts of threatened client behavior than others. The null hypothesis may be stated as follows: there are no differences among leader techniques in the amount of threatened client behavior which follow them. To test this hypothesis, the quality of client responses immediately following specific leader techniques was examined.

The first step required obtaining a measure of threatened client behavior. This involved selecting those client categories indicating that a member found it necessary to defend his self organization. Since the concept of threatened client behavior was to be used by the other investigators participating in this joint research, the problem was approached cooperatively. By common agreement the following client categories, indicative of threatened behavior, were selected: ambivalent acceptance of interpretation, rejection of clarification, expressions of confusion, defensive remarks, and deflection of the topic being discussed. Frequencies in these so-called threatened categories were compared with frequencies in all other client categories immediately following specific types of group leader behavior.

Through the use of t-test analysis, paired comparisons were made between all possible combinations of the following group leader techniques: simple acceptance, restatement of content, clarification of feeling, and pause. In no case was a value of t obtained which would allow the rejection of the null hypothesis. Consequently, at least in this study, there does not seem to be a specific leader category which is consistently followed by less threatened client behavior. It is possible that future research studies may be able to deal more adequately with this important issue. More definitive knowledge concerning leader behavior and threatened client behavior would greatly enhance our understanding of group psychotherapy.

The clinical experience of the writer led him to believe that when a group leader clarifies a negative feeling toward the self, defensive or threatened client behavior is more likely to result than when the clarification of feeling is more general. In this case the hypothesis is formulated as follows: there is no difference between "clarification of feeling" (general) and "clarification of negative feelings toward the self" in their being followed by threatened client responses. To test this hypothesis, client responses immediately following leader categories "clarification of feeling" (general) and "clarification of negative feelings toward the self" were tabulated in terms of threatened client behavior.

From these data a value of t was obtained which could easily have occurred through the accidents of sampling. The null hypothesis is not refuted. Therefore, there is no evidence that more threatened client behavior follows a clarification of negative feelings toward the self, and it is concluded that the clinical impression of the investigator is not confirmed by the data.

Therapeutic Gain and Threatened Client Behavior

One of the basic constructs of nondirective theory asserts that the absence of threat is conducive to personal change. Consequently, it should be expected that those group members who respond to leader techniques with a smaller proportion of threatened behavior are likely to be found in the group who benefited most from the experience.

Tabulation of frequencies confirmed this impression inasmuch as threatened client behavior following group leader techniques in the least-profited group is almost twice as great as in the most-profited group.

It seemed appropriate to examine the possibility that certain leader techniques showed significant differences in the amount of threatened behavior which followed them in the two "gained" groups. However, when each of the four major leader categories was examined with respect to the amount of threatened behavior which followed it in the two "gained" groups, none of the mean differences resulted in a t value which was significant at the

5 percent level of confidence. Consequently, the null hypothesis cannot be refuted, and it is concluded that no real differences exist.

GROUP LEADER FEELINGS TOWARD THE MEMBERS

Original plans called for a statistical analysis between similar items on the sociometric technique (the group analysis sheet) and a leader questionnaire (group leader feelings toward the members). This procedure proved impossible since the sociometric technique had to be withdrawn for reasons outlined in Chapter III. However, it seems profitable to describe the data obtained from the leader questionnaire and, in a qualitative manner, compare them with other findings in this study. It is realized that this is an inconclusive procedure, but the results are presented with the hope that they may provide valuable clues for future research in nondirective group psychotherapy.

Almost without exception the three group leaders mentioned members in the most-profited group among those with whom they seemed able to apply nondirective techniques most easily and, conversely, members in the least-profited group were almost invariably named among those felt most difficult to interact with nondirectively. This finding, if verified in subsequent groups, might have important prognostic implications. It seems worthy of further research of a more controlled nature.

The third and fourth items of the leader questionnaire required each leader to rank the members in his group according to his interpersonal comfort with them and, again, in terms of the relative amount of liking for each member. As one might expect, these two rankings, for any one group, were almost identical. That is, the leaders tend to like most those people with whom they feel most comfortable. Interestingly enough, those members who were assigned the highest ranking in the three groups were also among those who were later judged to have profited most from the experience. Any attempt to explain this apparent relationship should also take into consideration the possibility that leaders may tend to like most those members with whom they interact nondirectively most easily. There may be a relationship between therapeutic gain and the leader's attitude toward the members, but this assumption is recognized as speculative since more rigorous analysis is indicated with appropriate consideration of the uncontrolled variables involved.

Another item on the group leader questionnaire required the leader to estimate which of his members liked him least and which liked him most. In the vast majority of cases the leaders named people who they believed liked them best and who were later judged among the most-profited. Conversely, those members who the leaders believed liked them least were later judged among those in the least-profited group. The data are too meager for anything but speculative assumptions, but the leader's feelings about how the members react toward him would seem to be a profitable area for further investigation.

CHAPTER VII

SUMMARY AND CONCLUSIONS

The present cooperative investigation was undertaken to study the process of nondirective group psychotherapy. The nature of group psychotherapy has hardly been studied systematically. Relevant testable hypotheses needed to be subjected to controlled analysis in an effort to state conclusions at greater levels of confidence than those which inhere in clinical observation.

Together the investigators attempted to shed light on the questions of group therapy by examining the process from three distinct points of view. Telschow restricted his efforts to an analysis of the leader's behavior and its correlates; Gorlow studied the behavior of members as therapists for one another; Hoch analyzed the therapy process itself with relation to specifiable variables.

In general, the procedure involved selecting the subjects for inclusion in nondirective group therapy, providing them with the therapeutic experience, and examining them before and after the experience with certain psychological tests. The subjects were drawn from the graduate student body of Teachers College, Columbia University. An intake interview was used to insure the genuine motivation of the participants. The only criterion for selection and inclusion in a therapy group was that the individual possess deep-felt concern about some area of personal difficulty. Seventeen individuals, whose problems ranged from extreme tension to apprehension over the possible recurrence of "nervous breakdowns," were finally selected and organized into three groups for psychotherapy. Two groups were composed of six people each, while a third group consisted of five people.

Three psychological tests were used in the investigation, and they were administered routinely to each individual both before and after the group experience: the Rorschach; an Incomplete-Sentences Test; a Self-Rating Checklist. The instruments were utilized to achieve measurements of group members in the variables of initial personal adjustment, anxiety, hostility, and gain from psychotherapy.

Before one could proceed to test hypotheses about the events of nondirective group psychotherapy, three problems were posed: (1) A method for quantifying transcribed therapy protocols had to be developed. (2) The initial personal adjustment of members had to be evaluated. (3) Members had to be separated into two groups, those who gained most from the experience as against those who gained little or not at all. A methodology possessing acceptable reliability was developed for the quantification of protocols. (Approximately twelve hundred pages of single-spaced typescript were involved in the study.) The approach recognized the dynamic play of group psychotherapy and made the process of member interaction amenable to study. Group leader judgments on the initial adjustment of members and their gain from the therapy experience proved to be of validity when the judgments were related to independent psychological test criteria.

In general terms each of the investigators focused on the "what," the "when," and the "why" of the group psychotherapy process. Specifically three basic questions were considered: (1) What seems to characterize nondirective group psychotherapy? (2) When in the course of a group's cycle of activity do various features occur? (3) Why do certain phenomena take place?

CHARACTERISTICS OF THE NONDIRECTIVE GROUP PSYCHOTHERAPY PROCESS

Some features are found to occur with sufficient regularity to make the nondirective group therapy cycle at least to an extent a predictable process. Significant in this connection are the following:

1. Verbally the three groups behave in highly similar fashion. When the verbal behaviors of the groups are tabulated and compared, statistically significant correlations are found among the groups considered as a whole.

2. On the other hand, the behavior of individual members

within each group is considerably more diverse. Typical patterns of verbal activity, however, are predictable in terms of such variables as degree of gain.

Patterns of activity can be predicted with reference to members' behavior as therapists as well as leaders' interaction with the group members.

3. Both the quality and the quantity of member-therapist behavior are related to certain variables:

a. Significant differences exist in the quality of member-therapist behavior with respect to the personality variables of initial personal adjustment, anxiety, and hostility; in general, the healthier, less anxious, less hostile individuals utilize relatively more member-therapist behavior of a positive variety and less behavior of a negative variety.

b. A significant relationship exists between the *quantity* of an individual's member-therapist participation and his Rorschach productivity (as measured by the number of responses given).

4. Similarly, various aspects of the group leader's behavior can be predicted:

a. By far the greater part of the group leader's responses (98 percent in the present instance) are clearly nondirective in character.

b. Group leaders consistently interact more frequently with the more active group members.

c. With respect to the quantity of client behavior following the major group leader techniques, the latter do not produce any differential consequences; when "pause" is considered a therapeutic technique, it alone among the group leader techniques results in a significantly greater amount of client responses.

d. With regard to the quality of client responses immediately following leader responses, "restatement of content" and "clarification of feeling" are consistently followed by a greater number of positive client responses than are the remaining group leader techniques.

Another feature predictable in nondirective group psychotherapy is that the most-profited members will behave differently from the least-profited members. Analysis of the data indicates such differences with respect to members' behavior as clients and therapists as well as with regard to the group leaders' interaction with them.

5. With respect to the behavior of members as clients, the following is noted:

a. Both most-profited and least-profited members look upon themselves and others in a more favorable light at the conclusion of therapy.

b. However, while least-profited members still retain much of their original negative outlook, most-profited members show a statistically significant decrease in this respect.

6. With regard to the behavior of members as therapists significant differences are also found between most-profited and least-profited members:

a. Individuals of the most-profited group use relatively more therapist behavior of the positive variety and less of the negative variety than do individuals in the least-profited group.

b. While the member-therapist behavior of the least-profited group does not change significantly in the course of therapy, that of the most-profited group is characterized by a statistically significant increase in activity reflecting positive behavior and a decrease in activity reflecting negative behavior.

7. The group leader's interaction with most-profited and least-profited members yields results in the expected direction:

a. Most-profited members react with more "release units" than do least-profited members to responses directed to them by the leader, but the differences are not statistically significant.

b. Most-profited members make more responses than do least-profited members to group leader statements—again, however, the differences are not statistically significant.

c. Finally, the quality of the group leader's verbal interaction with most-profited and least-profited members is similar.

TEMPORAL ASPECTS OF THE NONDIRECTIVE GROUP THERAPY PROCESS

Essentially what one finds in analyzing the nondirective group therapy process as a function of time is that the behavior of members changes appreciably while that of the group leader remains fairly consistent. The following are noted:

1. Members behave differently in the second half of the therapy cycle in the following respects:

a. Client behavior of a positive nature is significantly more in evidence, reflecting presumably a healthier orientation toward life and people.

b. Client behavior of a negative variety shows a concomitant decline, although the decrease is not statistically significant.

c. In terms of progression, the graphs of positive emotion show a rather consistently rising trend in the course of the therapy cycle. The expression of negative emotion, on the other hand, reaches its peak during the middle of the therapy cycle and subsequently declines.

2. As therapists for one another, members reveal a corresponding change of behavior:

a. Member-therapist activity of a distinctly positive kind increases during the second half of therapy, while behavior of a negative variety decreases.

b. Comparison of member-therapist behavior in the first and last quarters of the therapy cycle reveals a statistically significant increase in nondirective behavior and a significant decrease in interpretive evaluative behavior as well as in interest in case material *per se.*

3. The behavior of the group leader, on the other hand, does not undergo any appreciable change in the course of the therapy cycle. Neither quantitatively nor qualitatively is his pattern of activity significantly different in the second half of therapy as compared with the first.

DYNAMICS OF THE NONDIRECTIVE GROUP PSYCHOTHERAPY PROCESS

The effort to account for certain phenomena observable in the course of nondirective group psychotherapy resulted in the following set of conclusions:

1. Discordant behavior is found to be related to the following variables:

a. It is less in evidence during discussion of themes in which several members show ego-involvement to the extent of their serving as clients and secondary clients.

b. It is less in evidence in groups in which members exhibit relatively similar patterns of verbal behavior.

c. It is less in evidence in those groups in which the leader is more active.

2. Additional findings indicated the need for a similar critical review of commonly accepted views concerning "insight" and its relation to "gain" in therapy. The present study disclosed the following:

a. The incidence of insightful remarks on the part of members is remarkably low, despite the fact that they profit from therapy.

b. The nature of such insight is more often of an epiphenomenal character rather than of the usually assumed sudden sensing of new relationships.

c. Most-profited members do not consistently voice more insight than do least-profited members.

3. A third major phenomenon—the degree of "threat" perceived by group members—was examined particularly with reference to its relation to the leader's behavior. Such conclusions as the following emerged:

a. There is no significant relationship between specific group leader techniques and the degree of threat accompanying them as revealed in the client's response.

b. Clarification of negative client feelings by the group leader does not induce significantly more threat in the client than does clarification of positive client feelings.

c. Although the difference is not statistically significant, least-profited members react to group leader statements with threatened behavior almost twice as often as do most-profited members.

4. The final consideration—factors underlying the nature of members' behavior during the therapy cycle—netted the following findings:

a. The statistically significant relationship between each member's behavior in the first two sessions and his behavior during the remainder of the therapy cycle suggests the feasibility of altering a group's composition on the basis of initial behavior.

b. While the quantity of member-therapist behavior cannot reliably be predicted from such personality attributes as initial personal adjustment, anxiety, and hostility, the quality of member-therapist behavior is associated with these variables; with statistically significant frequency the healthier, less anxious, less hostile members use more therapist behavior of a positive variety and less of a negative variety.

c. The initial health or adjustment of a member, on the other hand, is not found to bear any significant relationship to the group leader's interaction with him.

d. What does appear to influence the leader's reaction in part is his feeling toward a given member (as measured by sociometric instruments).

5. With regard to the type of member-therapist behavior displayed within the group, the following is noted:

a. The quality of a specific member-therapist's behavior toward another group member is associated with his personal feelings toward the member. Behavior directed toward a "liked" member is significantly different from behavior directed toward a "disliked" member. The former behavior is characterized by relatively more acceptance and permissiveness, and less evaluation and criticism.

b. The quality of member-therapist behavior differentiates the quality of client behavior. Therapist behavior of a positive variety induces exploration of the client problem, while therapist behavior of a negative variety induces personality defense and constriction.

With reference to the findings, the limitations of this type of investigation must be restated at this point. It should be added that the present investigation has examined the group psychotherapy process only as it is represented in verbal symbols. The latter may or may not reflect the unexpressed or subvocal accompaniments of interaction, an area being currently explored by Vermilye [96]. On the other hand, a consistent effort has been made to exploit the possibilities inherent in such verbal behavior data. Thus, the verbatim typescripts included wherever possible such references to the actual session as inflection of the speaker, tempo of speech, tone of voice, speed of delivery, length of pauses, and the like. Too, many of the sessions were observed from a one-way vision room for purposes of noting the tenor of interaction.

Finally, where a typescript section was ambiguous on any count, its categorization was accomplished by a replaying of the original recording.

In consequence, it is felt that the present study is one of the first to furnish a fairly specific picture of the dynamics of the group psychotherapy process as it appears under relatively controlled conditions. The product is the more meaningful in view of the cooperative nature of the research.

It should be pointed out that the interaction analysis currently being conducted at the Harvard Laboratory of Social Relations represents a thoroughgoing attempt to develop a general methodology for the study of group processes. As originally conceived, the present joint study included a fourth investigator, who was to have analyzed the data from that frame of reference. Had this aspect of the investigation materialized, it would undoubtedly have lent the study as a whole greater meaning.

In summary, then, the present study does not pretend to offer conclusive answers to the questions raised. Its contribution to our knowledge of what actually takes place in a group therapy process is rather of a path-pointing nature. Employing an original protocol analysis technique, the study has attempted to delimit a wide area of investigation by (a) furnishing tentative answers to broad questions, and (b) pointing up those aspects of group psychotherapy which merit intensive research.

BIBLIOGRAPHY

BIBLIOGRAPHY

1. ABRAHAMS, J. and McCORKLE, L. W. "Group Psychotherapy of Military Offenders." *The American Journal of Sociology,* 51: 455–464, 1946.
2. ACKERMAN, N. W. "Group Therapy from the Viewpoint of a Psychiatrist." *American Journal of Orthopsychiatry,* 12: 678–690, 1943.
3. ACKERMAN, N. W. "Some Theoretical Aspects of Group Psychotherapy." In J. L. Moreno (Ed.), *Group Psychotherapy: A Symposium.* New York: Beacon House, 1945.
4. ALPERT, A. "Education as Therapy." *Psychoanalytic Quarterly,* 10: 468–474, 1941.
5. AMSTER, F. "Collective Psychotherapy of Mothers of Emotionally Disturbed Children." *American Journal of Orthopsychiatry,* 14: 44–53, 1944.
6. BARUCH, D. W. "Description of a Project in Group Therapy." *Journal of Consulting Psychology,* 9: 271–280, 1945.
7. BARUCH, D. W. and MILLER, H. "Group and Individual Psychotherapy as an Adjunct in the Treatment of Allergy." *Journal of Consulting Psychology,* 10: 281–284, 1946.
8. BELL, J. E. *Projective Techniques.* New York: Longmans, Green and Co., Inc., 1948.
9. BENDER, L. "Group Activities on a Children's Ward as Methods of Psychotherapy." *The American Journal of Psychiatry,* 93: 1151–1173, 1937.
10. BIXBY, F. L. *et al.* "The Application of the Group Method to the Classification of Prisoners." In J. L. Moreno (Ed.), *Group Psychotherapy: A Symposium.* New York: Beacon House, 1945.
11. BLACKMAN, N. "Ward Therapy: A New Method of Group Psychotherapy." *Psychiatric Quarterly,* 16: 660–666, 1942.
12. BRACELAND, F. J. "Group Psychotherapy." In J. L. Moreno (Ed.), *Group Psychotherapy: A Symposium.* New York: Beacon House, 1945.
13. BUCK, R. W. "The Class Method in the Treatment of Essential Hypertension." *Annals of Internal Medicine,* 11: 511–518, 1937.
14. CARR, A. C. "A Coordinated Research in Psychotherapy: Evaluation of Nine Psychotherapy Cases by the Rorschach." *Journal of Consulting Psychology,* 13: 196–205, 1949.
15. CHAPPELL, M. N. *et al.* "The Value of Group Psychological Procedures in the Treatment of Peptic Ulcer." *American Journal of Digestive Diseases and Nutrition,* 3: 813–817, 1937.
16. COHEN, R. C. Military Group Psychotherapy. *Mental Hygiene,* 31: 94–102, 1947.

17. CURRAN, C. A. *Personality Factors in Counseling.* New York: Grune & Stratton, 1945.
18. CURRAN, F. J. and SCHILDER, P. "A Constructive Approach to the Problems of Childhood and Adolescence." *Journal of Criminal Psychopathology,* 2: 125–142, 305–320, 1940–1941.
19. DEWAR, M. C. "The Technique of Group Therapy." *Bulletin of the Menninger Clinic,* 10: 82–84, 1946.
20. DURKIN, H. E. *et al.* "Therapy of Mothers in Groups." *American Journal of Orthopsychiatry,* 14: 68–76, 1944.
21. ELIZUR, A. *Content Analysis of the Rorschach with Regard to Anxiety and Hostility.* Unpublished Ph.D. thesis, Teachers College, Columbia University, 1949.
22. FLEMING, L. and SNYDER, W. U. "Social and Personal Changes Following Nondirective Group Play Therapy." *American Journal of Orthopsychiatry,* 17: 101–116, 1947.
23. FOULKES, S. H. *Introduction to Group-Analytic Psychotherapy.* London: William Heinemann Medical Books, Ltd., 1948.
24. FOULKES, S. H. "On Group Analysis." *International Journal of Psycho-Analysis,* 27: 46–51, 1946.
25. GABRIEL, B. "Group Treatment for Adolescent Girls." *American Journal of Orthopsychiatry,* 14: 593–602, 1944.
26. GLATZER, H. T. and DURKIN, H. E. "The Role of the Therapist in Group Relationship Therapy." *The Nervous Child,* 4: 243–251, 1945.
27. GORLOW, L. *Nondirective Group Psychotherapy: An Analysis of the Behavior of Members as Therapists.* Unpublished Ph.D. thesis, Teachers College, Columbia University, 1950.
28. GROTJAHN, M. "Experience with Group Psychotherapy as a Method of Treatment for Veterans." *The American Journal of Psychiatry,* 103: 637–643, 1947.
29. HADDEN, S. B. "Post-military Group Psychotherapy with Psychoneurotics." *Mental Hygiene,* 31: 89–93, 1947.
30. HADDEN, S. B. "The Utilization of a Therapy Group in Teaching Psychotherapy." *The American Journal of Psychiatry,* 103: 644–648, 1947.
31. HADDEN, S. B. "Treatment of the Neuroses by Class Technic." *Annals of Internal Medicine,* 16: 33–37, 1942.
32. HARTWELL, S. W. *et al.* "The Application of the Group Method to the Classification of Prisoners." In J. L. Moreno (Ed.), *Group Psychotherapy: A Symposium.* New York: Beacon House, 1945.
33. HILDRETH, H. M. "A Battery of Feeling and Attitude Scales for Clinical Use." *Journal of Clinical Psychology,* 2: 214–221, 1946.
34. HOBBS, N. "Insight in Short-Term Psychotherapy." *The American Psychologist,* 4: 273, 1949 (Abstract).
35. HOBBS, N. *Psychological Research and Services in an Army Air Forces Convalescent Hospital.* Unpublished Ph.D. thesis, Ohio State University, 1946.

36. Hobbs, N. and Pascal, G. "A Method for the Quantitative Analysis of Group Psychotherapy." *The American Psychologist*, 1: 297, 1946.

37. Horwitz, S. "The Spontaneous Drama as a Technic in Group Therapy." *The Nervous Child*, 4: 252–273, 1945.

38. Kadis, A. L. and Lazarsfeld, S. "The Group as a Psychotherapeutic Factor in Counseling Work." *The Nervous Child*, 4: 228–235, 1945.

39. Karpman, B. *et al.* "The Application of the Group Method to the Classification of Prisoners." In J. L. Moreno (Ed.), *Group Psychotherapy: A Symposium*. New York: Beacon House, 1945.

40. Klapman, J. W. "An Observation on the Interrelationship of Group and Individual Psychotherapy." *Journal of Nervous and Mental Disease*, 101: 242–246, 1945.

41. Klapman, J. W. *Group Psychotherapy: Theory and Practice*. New York: Grune & Stratton, 1946.

42. Klopfer, W. G. "The Efficacy of Group Therapy as Indicated by Group Rorschach Records." *Rorschach Research Exchange*, 9: 207–209, 1945.

43. Kolodney, E. "Treatment of Mothers in Groups as a Supplement to Child Psychotherapy." *Mental Hygiene*, 28: 437–444, 1944.

44. Lawlor, G. W. "Psychodrama in Group Therapy." *Sociometry*, 9: 275–281, 1946.

45. Lazell, E. W. "Group Psychotherapy." In J. L. Moreno (Ed.), *Group Psychotherapy: A Symposium*. New York: Beacon House, 1945.

46. Lazell, E. W. "The Group Treatment of Dementia Praecox." *Psychoanalytic Review*, 8: 168–179, 1921.

47. Little, H. M. and Konopka, G. "Group Therapy in a Child Guidance Center." *American Journal of Orthopsychiatry*, 17: 303–311, 1947.

48. Lowrey, L. G. "Group Treatment for Mothers." *American Journal of Orthopsychiatry*, 14: 589–592, 1944.

49. Luchins, A. S. "A Course in Group Psychotherapy; Method, Content, and Results." *Journal of Clinical Psychology*, 2: 231–239, 1946.

50. Marquis, D. G. "Research Planning at the Frontiers of Science." *The American Psychologist*, 3: 430–438, 1948.

51. Marsh, L. C. "Group Therapy and the Psychiatric Clinic." *Journal of Nervous and Mental Disease*, 82: 381–393, 1935.

52. Meiers, J. I. "Origins and Development of Group Psychotherapy." In J. L. Moreno (Ed.), *Group Psychotherapy: A Symposium*. New York: Beacon House, 1945.

53. Moreno, J. L. "Scientific Foundations of Group Psychotherapy." In J. L. Moreno (Ed.), *Group Psychotherapy: A Symposium*. New York: Beacon House, 1945.

54. Moreno, J. L. "The Application of the Group Method to the Classification of Prisoners." In J. L. Moreno (Ed.), *Group Psychotherapy: A Symposium*. New York: Beacon House, 1945.

55. Moreno, J. L. and Toeman, Z. "The Group Approach in Psychodrama." *Sociometry*, 5: 191–194, 1942.

56. MUENCH, G. A. *An Evaluation of Nondirective Psychotherapy by Means of the Rorschach and Other Indices.* Applied Psychology Monographs, No. 13. Stanford University, California: Stanford University Press, 1947.

57. PEDERSON-KRAG, G. "Unconscious Factors in Group Therapy." *Psychoanalytic Quarterly,* 15: 180–189, 1946.

58. PERES, H. "An Investigation of Nondirective Group Therapy." *Journal of Consulting Psychology,* 11: 159–172, 1947.

59. PORTER, E. H. "The Development and Evaluation of a Measure of Counseling Interview Procedures." *Educational and Psychological Measurement,* 3: 105–126, 215–238, 1943.

60. PRATT, J. H. "The Home Sanatorium Treatment of Consumption." *Bulletin of the Johns Hopkins Hospital,* 17: 140–158, 1906.

61. PROSHANSKY, H. and MURPHY, G. "The Effects of Reward and Punishment on Perception." *The Journal of Psychology,* 13: 295–305, 1942.

62. RAIMY, V. R. *The Self-Concept as a Factor in Counseling and Personality Organization.* Unpublished Ph.D. thesis, Ohio State University, 1943.

63. RASKIN, N. J. "Development of the Parallel Studies Project." *Journal of Consulting Psychology,* 13: 149–220, 1949.

64. READER, N. *An Investigation into Some Personality Changes Occurring in Individuals Undergoing Client-Centered Therapy.* Unpublished Ph.D. thesis, University of Chicago, 1948.

65. REDL, F. "Group Emotion and Leadership." *Psychiatry,* 5: 573–596, 1942.

66. ROGERS, C. R. "A Coordinated Research in Psychotherapy: A Nonobjective Introduction." *Journal of Consulting Psychology,* 13: 149–153, 1949.

67. ROGERS, C. R. *Counseling and Psychotherapy: Newer Concepts in Practice.* Boston: Houghton Mifflin Co., 1942.

68. ROYER, A. E. *An Analysis of Counseling Procedures in a Nondirective Approach.* Unpublished Master's thesis, Ohio State University, 1943.

69. RUBIN, H. E. and KATZ, E. "Auroratone Films for the Treatment of Psychotic Depressions in an Army General Hospital." *Journal of Clinical Psychology,* 2: 333–340, 1946.

70. SANFORD, R. N. "The Effects of Abstinence from Food upon Imaginal Processes." *The Journal of Psychology,* 2: 129–136, 1936.

71. SARLIN, C. N. and BEREZIN, M. A. "Group Psychotherapy on a Modified Analytic Basis." *Journal of Nervous and Mental Disease,* 104: 611–667, 1946.

72. SCHAFER, R. and MURPHY, G. "The Role of Autism in a Visual Figure–Ground Relationship." *Journal of Experimental Psychology,* 32: 335–343, 1943.

73. SCHAUER, G. "Patients as Therapeutic Agents in a Mental Hospital." In J. L. Moreno (Ed.), *Group Phychotherapy: A Symposium.* New York, Beacon House, 1945.

74. SCHILDER, P. "Introductory Remarks on Groups." *The Journal of Social Psychology,* 12: 83–100, 1940.

75. SCHILDER, P. *Psychotherapy.* New York: W. W. Norton & Co., Inc., 1938.

76. SCHILDER, P. "Results and Problems of Group Psychotherapy in Severe Neuroses." *Mental Hygiene,* 23: 87–99, 1939.

77. SCHWARTZ, L. A. "Group Psychotherapy in the War Neuroses." *The American Journal of Psychiatry,* 101: 498–500, 1945.

78. SEEMAN, J. "A Study of the Process of Nondirective Therapy." *Journal of Consulting Psychology,* 13: 157–168, 1949.

79. SHAFFER, L. F. "The Problem of Psychotherapy. *The American Psychologist,* 2: 459–467, 1947.

80. SHASKAN, D. A. "Must Individual and Group Psychotherapy Be Opposed?" *American Journal of Orthopsychiatry,* 17: 290–292, 1947.

81. SIMON, B. *et al.* "Group Therapy from the Viewpoint of the Patient." *Journal of Nervous and Mental Disease,* 105: 156–170, 1946.

82. SLAVSON, S. R. *An Introduction to Group Therapy.* New York: Commonwealth Fund, 1943.

83. SLAVSON, S. R. "Differential Dynamics of Activity and Interview Group Therapy. *"American Journal of Orthopsychiatry,* 17: 293–302, 1947.

84. SLAVSON, S. R. "Differential Methods of Group Therapy in Relation to Age Levels." *The Nervous Child,* 4: 196–210, 1945.

85. SLAVSON, S. R. (Ed.). *The Practice of Group Therapy.* New York: International Universities Press, 1947.

86. SLAVSON, S. R. *et al.* "Activity Group Therapy with a Delinquent Dull Boy of Eleven." *The Nervous Child,* 4: 274–290, 1945.

87. SNOWDEN, E. "Mass Psychotherapy." *Lancet,* 2: 769–770, 1940.

88. SNYDER, W. U. "An Investigation of the Nature of Non-directive Psychotherapy." *The Journal of General Psychology,* 33: 193–223, 1945.

89. SNYDER, W. U. (Ed.). *Casebook of Nondirective Therapy.* Boston: Houghton Mifflin Co., 1947.

90. SNYGG, D. and COMBS, A. W. *Individual Behavior.* New York: Harper and Brothers, 1949.

91. SOLBY, B. "Group Psychotherapy and the Psychodramatic Method." In J. L. Moreno (Ed.), *Group Psychotherapy: A Symposium.* New York: Beacon House, 1945.

92. SOLOMON, J. C. and AXELROD, P. L. "Group Psychotherapy for Withdrawn Adolescents." *American Journal of Diseases of Children,* 68: 86–101, 1944.

93. STEWART, K. K. and AXELROD, P. L. "Group Therapy on a Children's Psychiatric Ward: Experiment Combining Group Therapy with Individual Therapy and Resident Treatment." *American Journal of Orthopsychiatry,* 17: 312–325, 1947.

94. THOMAS, G. W. "Group Psychotherapy: A Review of the Recent Literature." *Psychosomatic Medicine,* 5: 166–180, 1943.

95. THOMPSON, M. *A Study of the Self-Concept in an Experience Conducive to Change.* Unpublished Ph.D. thesis, Teachers College, Columbia University, 1949.

96. VERMILYE, D. W. *Description and Analysis of a Specific Type of Non-*

verbal Behavior in a Group Situation. Unpublished Ph.D. thesis, Teachers College, Columbia University. (In preparation)

97. WENDER, L. "The Dynamics of Group Psychotherapy and Its Application." *Journal of Nervous and Mental Disease,* 84: 54–60, 1936.

98. WENDER, L. "Group Psychotherapy." In J. L. Moreno (Ed.), *Group Psychotherapy: A Symposium.* New York: Beacon House, 1945.

99. WHITE, H. C. "An Adventure in Group Therapy in a Family-Agency Setting." *Mental Hygiene,* 28: 422–430, 1944.

100. WHITE, W. A. "Proposal of a Plan of Group Psychotherapy." In J. L. Moreno (Ed.), *Group Psychotherapy: A Symposium.* New York: Beacon House, 1945.

101. WOLF, A. "Group Analysis." An address delivered before the American Group Psychotherapy Conference. New York, 1948.

APPENDICES

APPENDIX A

DEFINITIONS AND EXAMPLES OF CATEGORIES OF ANALYSIS *

C1 Discussion of Plans (A client statement indicating a positive course of action to be undertaken). "Realizing this about myself, I'm going to make a real effort to get in with more people and attend the Friday night square dance regularly."

C2 Insight and Understanding (A client statement indicating newly perceived relationships which help him in self-understanding). "I just realized it. I never thought of it before but what I have been doing has been to try to gain approval from everybody."

C3 Positive Attitude Toward Self (A client statement indicating a positive feeling toward some aspect of his own personality). "I realize now that I have more ability than I thought I had."

C4 Positive Attitude Toward Others (A client statement indicating a positive feeling toward others in the environment). "I understand my mother better now and I feel more warmly toward her."

C5 Ambivalent Acceptance of Self (A client statement indicating conflicting feelings toward his own personality). "I feel somewhat better about my reaction to new people but I'm still not completely satisfied with my social adjustment."

C6 Ambivalent Acceptance of Others (A client statement indicating conflicting feelings about someone in the environment). "He has a lot of good qualities but at the same time I can't help but feel resentment toward him. Maybe he is a good guy after all."

C7 Statement of Problem (A client statement about an area of concern to him). "Ah, I was waiting to hear from the others first because it seems to me my problem is more acute than the rest of the problems . . . it is acute in the sense that it is an emotional problem which seems to have physical symptoms. . . ."

C8 Elaboration of Problem (Client statements which expand or elaborate on the originally stated problem).

---

* These categories have been in part devised by the present authors and in part taken over from "An Investigation of the Nature of Non-directive Psychotherapy" (*The Journal of General Psychology*, 33:193–223, 1945) by permission of the author, W. U. Snyder.

125

C9 Acceptance of Clarification (A client statement indicating acceptance of the reformulation of his own statement by a member-therapist or a group leader). "That's right. And as a result you wake up the next day and you are, you know—you just feel terrible."

C10 Acceptance of Opinion, Advice (A client statement that seems to indicate that the opinion expressed by a member-therapist is acceptable). "Yes, I can see that's right."

C11 Acceptance of Interpretation (A client statement indicating acceptance of a member-therapist's interpretative remark). "Oh, I'm very much inclined to think so. All of us need more affection than we are getting in our relationships."

C12 Ambivalent Acceptance of Clarification (A client statement indicating partial acceptance of a member-therapist's or group leader's attempt to reformulate his own view of things or clarify the feeling involved). "No, I don't think that quite expresses how I feel about it."

C13 Ambivalent Acceptance of Opinion, Advice (A client statement indicating partial acceptance of a member-therapist expression of opinion or advice). "Well, I think maybe that is a good idea but it would be hard for me to do."

C14 Ambivalent Acceptance of Interpretation (A client statement indicating partial acceptance of a member-therapist's interpretative remark). "Well, that might be the case but I'll have to think about it some more."

C15 Rejection of Interpretation (A client statement indicating non-acceptance of a member-therapist remark of an interpretative nature). "No, I don't believe that explains it at all in my case."

C16 Rejection of Opinion, Advice (A client response indicating that the opinion of a member-therapist is not acceptable to him). "Well, what bearing—what bearing would that have on the situation—I still don't see the direct connection."

C17 Rejection of Clarification (A client statement indicating nonacceptance of a member-therapist's or group leader's statement reformulating the essential content or feeling of his own statement). "No, that is not the way I feel."

C18 Confusion, Asking for Help (A client statement indicating confusion about some aspect of his personality and/or requesting aid from the other members). "That is what I'm wondering now, the purpose of my being "goody-goody" all my life, you know."

C19 Defensive Remarks (Client responses indicating threatened behavior as a result of member-therapist comments). "That sounds very terrible, but I accept it without analyzing it and so actually I feel it's good . . . as a fact, it has kept me much healthier than a lot of people around me."

C20 Deflection (A client response indicating a desire to deflect the topic of conversation away from himself). "Well, let's stop this and go on to somebody else."

C21 Negative Attitude Toward Others (A client statement indicating negative attitude toward others in the environment). "I resent my mother's trying to manage my life."

C22 Negative Attitude Toward Self (A client response indicating a negative attitude toward some personal quality). "And I was too timid, I wouldn't fight for myself so my older sister did that for me."

T1 Clarification of Feeling (A member-therapist response which attempts to clarify the feeling expressed by a client). "You feel encouraged by your behavior in that situation."

T2 Restatement of Content (An attempt by a member-therapist to demonstrate understanding of the client by restating the essential content of his remarks). "You don't relax when you sleep like that, that's why you are so tired."

T3 Simple Acceptance (A member-therapist response which indicates acceptance of a client statement without evaluation). "I see. I understand."

T4 Nondirective Lead (A member-therapist remark which stimulates client exploration of a problem but permits the direction to be chosen by the client). "Who has a problem that he feels like discussing today?"

T5 Structuring (A member-therapist statement defining the therapeutic situation). "Our time is just about up today; maybe we can continue this next time."

T6 Clarifying Question (A member-therapist statement indicating incomplete understanding and requesting further elaboration). "I don't quite understand what you mean."

T7 Empathy (A member-therapist remark indicating a "feeling with" the client based on similar experiences). "Having felt the same way myself, I know how you must have reacted to this."

T8 Approval, Encouragement (A member-therapist response indicating approval of client's views). "Yes, that sounds like a good idea."

T9 Reassurance (A member-therapist remark which attempts to reassure a client). "Most people have that trouble."

T10 Opinion (A statement of a member-therapist expressing his own opinion about the situation the client is in). "Don't you feel that you can have a friendship relationship with a girl until such time as you are able to get married?"

T10W Counter-opinion (A member-therapist remark indicating disagreement with another member-therapist's opinion of a situation). "I don't think that's a good idea at all. I think she should go to her mother and talk this over."

T11 Requesting Client to Elaborate (An attempt by a member-therapist to force client to develop a line of discussion). "I was wondering, Mildred, what your reactions were to what we talked about last time . . . is there anything you can tell us about how you felt afterwards and so on."

T12 Persuasion, Suggestion, Advice (An attempt by a member-therapist to suggest a course of action to a client). "What is to stop you from transferring to some hospital work or clinical work up in Connecticut where you are going to live?"

T13 Interpretation (A member-therapist remark which points out cause-and-effect relationships not expressed by the client). "Basically you like to be flattered . . . like to be shown love but you for some reason can't accept it."

T14 Deflection (A member-therapist remark indicating an effort to steer the focus of attention away from the present client). "Let's let this go for a while. Does anybody else have something he would like to talk about?"

T15 Evaluation (A remark by a member-therapist which evaluates the client's attack upon a situation). "Ah, another thing that suggests itself is that you haven't thought about marriage as realistically as you might."

T16 Disapproval, Criticism (A member-therapist remark which is openly critical of a client's behavior). "It would hardly seem to be a good friendship relationship and I think that's bad."

G1 Comparing Experiences. "I had a similar reaction when I was in a situation like that. Let me tell you about it."

G2 Proposing Course of Group Action. "I think it might be a good idea if we went around in a circle and told our problems."

G3 Posing Question for Group. "What do all of you think about Karen Horney's book about neurotic people? Have you read it?"

G4 Giving Information, Answering a Question. "That book is in the library and if you want it you can read it there."

G5 Friendly Discussion. "How's your course coming along?"

G6 Intellectual Discussion, Opinion. "Well, I feel that freedom lies within ourselves, rather than in the outside forces."

G6W Intellectual Counter-discussion, Counter-opinion. "I would like to share your optimistic view, but what I see now in our world is that there is a great deal of injustice."

G7 Humor (laughing). "I guess none of us has any problems today."

G8 Asking Group Leader a Question. "You're trained in this field. Why do *you* think I keep doing these things?"

APPENDIX B

INCOMPLETE-SENTENCES TEST *
(Form TC-S)

Number   Date

Complete these sentences to express how you really feel. Work rapidly and try to be fully frank. Sometimes a word will suffice to complete your idea; sometimes a phrase or a sentence will best convey your thought. Try to reveal as much of your feelings as you can.

1. I like_____
2. At night_____
3. Children_____
4. School is_____
5. Other people_____
6. I hate_____
7. I wish_____
8. My mother_____
9. Men are_____
10. My life_____
11. I need_____
12. The best_____
13. When I'm alone_____
14. My work_____
15. Marriage is_____
16. My health_____
17. What annoys me is_____
18. My father_____
19. Sexual relationships_____
20. My ambition is_____
21. The worst_____

* The Incomplete-Sentences Test (Form TC-S) was devised by Professor Nicholas Hobbs for use in a group therapy research program at Teachers College, Columbia University. Certain items which appeared in the Incomplete Sentence Test, DE303A, developed by Julian B. Rotter and Benjamin Willerman and described on pp. 150–51 of AAF Aviation Psychology Research Report No. 15, *The Psychological Program in AAF Convalescent Hospitals* (Washington, D.C., 1947), are included above and quoted here by permission of the authors.

129

22. Studying_____
23. I avoid_____
24. My nerves_____
25. I consider myself to be_____
26. Dirty_____
27. I fear_____
28. My mind_____
29. My home_____
30. I regret_____
31. Most women_____
32. The future_____
33. As a child, I_____
34. What thrills me is_____
35. Drinking_____
36. My disposition_____
37. Few people know that I_____
38. I am proudest of_____
39. I get depressed_____
40. I am closest to_____
41. People consider me_____
42. I look forward to_____
43. I am ashamed of_____
44. I wish people would_____
45. My worst fault is_____
46. I feel_____
47. I sometimes think_____
48. My biggest worry_____
49. My greatest joy_____
50. Secretly_____

APPENDIX C

SELF-RATING CHECKLIST *

Number   (Form DB-2)   Date

Check the statement which comes nearest to describing how you feel most of the time:

—Bursting with energy
—Full of pep
—Takes quite a bit to tire me out
—More than average energy
—Have a fair amount of energy
—Not too much pep but I can keep going
—Don't seem to have much energy
—Tired most of the time
—Worn out
—Completely worn out

Check the statement which comes nearest to describing how you feel most of the time:

—Full of enthusiasm
—Everything's working out fine
—The future doesn't look too bad
—Can't complain
—Get discouraged once in a while
—Uncertain about the future
—Insecure
—Dissatisfied with everything
—Can't stand much more
—No hope

Check the statement which comes nearest to describing how you feel most of the time:

—I am usually beautifully dressed and groomed; very attractive in appearance.
—My appearance is more attractive than that of the great majority of women.
—I consider my personal appearance quite satisfactory
—In most respects my appearance is all right.
—I guess I look as well as the average woman.
—I don't seem to look as well as most women.
—Except for a few good points, my appearance is unattractive.
—I don't like the way I look at all.

Check the statement which you think describes you best at the present time:

—I'm operating with maximum efficiency.
—I'm pretty close to my top level.
—I'm functioning on a fairly high level.
—As a general rule, I give a fair account of myself.
—I guess I could do somewhat better.
—I know I'm not doing as good a job as I could.
—I'm operating quite below my capacity.
—My usual performance is far below what I'm capable of.
—I'm pretty close to my lowest level.
—I'm not accomplishing one percent of what I really could.

* Adapted from "A Battery of Feeling and Attitude Scales for Clinical Use" (*Journal of Clinical Psychology*, 2:214–221, 1946) by permission of the author, H. M. Hildreth.

Check the statement which you think describes you best at the present time:

—I have no trouble in sizing up situations.
—I'm able to keep my head in tight spots.
—My judgment is usually pretty good.
—Usually I don't have much trouble thinking.
—It seems I think very slowly.
—I can't stop thinking about myself.
—I'm often confused and don't know what I'm doing.
—My mind is so mixed up, I don't know whether I'm coming or going.

Check the statement which you think describes you best at the present time:

—I like to finish a job, even though it means staying on a little late.
—Even though I don't like the job, I usually do it pretty thoroughly.
—I can get interested enough in most jobs so that I can do fairly decent work at them.
—I do most jobs just about as thoroughly as the average person.
—I take it easy, but I manage to get it done.
—I get the job done all right, but I never push myself.
—I'll work, but I've got to rest often in order to keep at any job.
—I can't do a job at all unless I'm in the mood for it.
—The longer I work at any job, the more angry I feel.

Check the statement which you think best describes you at the present time:

—I get along fine with everybody.
—I like most everyone I meet.
—On the whole, I feel friendly toward others.
—Some people I like, some I don't.
—I feel indifferent to most people.
—I don't get along with others very well.
—Most people irritate me.
—I can't stand people.
—I hate everything and everybody.

Check the statement which you think best describes you at the present time:

—It's easy for me to get along with everyone.
—I get along with most everyone.
—I feel cooperative toward others most of the time.
—I take people as I find them.
—I'm pretty sensitive about what other people think of me.
—Nobody pays much attention to what I do or say.
—Nobody understands me.
—Most of the time I'm mad at everybody.
—I hate the world.

Check the statement which you think describes you best at the present time:

—I'm one of those fortunate people who just have no problems.
—I have no problems worth mentioning.
—What few problems I do have cause me no trouble at all.
—Very few of my problems are serious.
—I have a few problems but will probably be able to solve them.
—Sometimes I wonder whether I'm able to solve certain of my problems.

Check the statement which comes nearest to describing how you feel at the present time:

—If society adopted the values which govern my life, we'd have a perfect world.
—Few people hold values as fine as mine.
—Most of my values are of a high caliber.
—For the most part I have a fairly good set of values.
—I guess my values are about like those of the average person.

—Some of my problems will probably have to go unsolved.

—Some of the things that bother me are pretty hard to bear.

—Mighty few people have troubles as serious as mine.

—With problems as serious as mine, I may soon give up completely.

—I'm afraid my values don't quite match those of the next fellow.

—I feel quite definitely the inadequacy of my values.

—What values I do have, don't count for much.

—If I have any values, they're worth next to nothing.

—Values just don't exist in my life.

Check the statement which you think describes you best at the present time:

—I doubt that anyone could possibly be better adjusted sexually that I am.

—My sexual adjustment is extremely satisfactory.

—In general, I think I'm well adjusted sexually.

—I suppose my sexual adjustment is about as good as that of most people.

—Sex causes very little trouble in my life.

—My sexual adjustment could stand improvement.

—I feel my sexual adjustment is inadequate.

—There's no doubt about it—sex is a real problem for me.

—The problem of sex causes me plenty of trouble.

—Sex is the most difficult problem I have to face.

Check the statement which you think describes you best at the present time:

—If all people were like me, the world would be a grand place.

—I think I'm better than the great majority of people.

—If I do say so myself, I have a very high opinion of my personal worth.

—In most respects I'm pretty good.

—I guess I'm worth about as much as the average person.

—Somehow I don't quite seem to measure up to the next fellow.

—I have a little worth, I guess.

—Except for a few good points, I'm not worth very much.

—If I died tomorrow, little would be lost.

—I'm completely useless.

Check the statement which you think describes your feelings best: ("Family": father, mother, brothers, sisters)

—My family relations are ideal in every respect.

—My relations with my family are extremely good.

—Usually my family and I get along fine.

—Except for occasional disagreements we get on well together.

—I guess most families have the kind of disagreements we have.

—Our disagreements get kind of serious at times.

—I find it quite difficult to stay on good terms with them.

—Frequently we're on bad terms with each other.

Check the statement which comes nearest to describing how you feel most of the time:

—I feel very capable of getting and keeping the attention of many men.

—I feel some men are attracted to me.

—I feel men do not usually notice me until they're well acquainted.

—I feel I have few masculine friends or admirers.

—I feel unattractive and uncomfortable with most men.

—My family is extremely difficult to get
along with.
—My family and I just never could get
along.

Check the statement which comes
nearest to describing how you feel
most of the time:

—I am very strong and vigorous; in
perfect health.
—I have average vitality; good health.
—I have some minor complaints; gen-
erally good health.
—I am rarely ill; but lacking in vitality.
—I suffer generally from poor health.

Check the statement which comes
nearest to describing how you feel
most of the time:

—I have no friends.
—I have a few acquaintances; no friends.
—I have one or two friends.
—I have a few good friends.
—I have many casual friends.
—I have many close friends.
—I have hundreds of friends.

APPENDIX D

GROUP ANALYSIS SHEET

Form A   Member No. —

1. Presently, I feel most comfortable with member No. —
2. Presently, I feel least comfortable with member No. —

3. The person most favorably disposed toward me is member No. —
4. The person least favorably disposed toward me is member No. —

5. The person who understands me most is member No. —
6. The person who understands me least is member No. —

7. The one who talks most freely about his problems is member No. —
8. The one who talks least freely about his problems is member No. —

9. The one who seems to profit most from this experience is member No. —
10. The one who seems to profit least from this experience is member No. —

11. The one who most helps me express myself is member No. —
12. The one who least helps me express myself is member No. —

13. Member No. — and member No. — understand each other best.
14. Member No. — and member No. — understand each other least.

15. Presently, I would rate each member of the group on the following scale:

    1 — severely upset   Member No. —
    2 — moderately upset   —
    3 — rather perturbed   —
    4 — relatively unperturbed   —
    5 — apparently free from stress   —

16. On the whole, this group seems to be (check one):
    — wasting time
    — getting ready to do some good
    — accomplishing something but in a very limited fashion
    — doing something pretty important for the participants

17. Thus far, my experience in the group has resulted in (check one):
    — no progress in the solution of my problems
    — some progress in their solution
    — considerable progress in their solution

---

18. Presently, my feelings toward the group leader are: (check appropriate items)

    — indifference to him   — warmly toward him
    — hostility toward him   — dependent on him
    — inhibited by him   — understood by him
    — respectful of him   — affection toward him
    — misunderstood by him

---

19. Presently, I think the group leader feels: (check appropriate items)

    — critical of me   — uninterested in me
    — hostile toward me   — affectionate toward me
    — respectful of me   — accepting of me
    — indifferent to me   — interested in me
    — warmly toward me

---

20. The person toward whom the group leader seems most favorably disposed is member No. —
21. The person toward whom the group leader seems least favorably disposed is member No. —

---

22. The person whom the group leader seems to understand best is member No. —
23. The person whom the group leader seems to understand least is member No. —

Since it is felt that you might have some need for expression outside the limits of this questionnaire, feel free to use the reverse side of this sheet for this purpose.

APPENDIX E

GROUP LEADER FEELINGS TOWARD THE MEMBERS

Form B

Group Leader ————————
Session No. ————————

I was able to apply N-D techniques most easily with member No. —
I was able to apply N-D techniques least easily with member No. —
I rank the members according to my interpersonal comfort with them ————
I liked the members (rank order) ————————————————
It seems to me that the member who talks most freely is No. —
It seems to me that the member who talks least freely is No. —
The member who seems to profit most is No. —
The member who seems to profit least is No. —
I rate group progress this session

(check one) Wasting time —
Getting ready to accomplish something —
Accomplishing something in limited way —
Important progress for participants —

It seems to me that the best member-therapist is No. —
It seems to me that the worst member-therapist is No. —
I rate each member as to his degree of upset on the following scale:

Severely upset ————————
Moderately upset ————————
Rather perturbed ————————
Relatively unperturbed ————
Apparently free from stress ——

The member who seems to like me least is No. —
The member who seems to like me most is No. —
Those members who seem to understand each other best are No. — and No. —
Those members who seem to understand each other least are No. — and No. —

INDEX

INDEX